GUT PUNCH

Is It Your Trauma or Intuition?

How to Cultivate a Safety State of Mind

BY DIANE SEAMARK

Published by Prominence Publishing.

ISBN: 978-1-997649-19-9

Trigger Warning

Throughout the book, I use examples involving students, clients, and drills I teach on-site at my academy, Sadohana. The language of these simulated scenarios can be triggering. You can absolutely skip this. There are many tools offered in this book, and you don't need to try and grasp every one of them now.

It will be important for you to revisit parts of the book as your healing develops. You do not enter into a level of healing work UNTIL you have built up enough capacity in your body. Your body includes your nervous system. To be able to level up and heal from the inside, you need to learn how to hold new levels of awareness. Give yourself grace and space as you learn these new skills.

Dedicated to Grandma Mary, who told me to never settle.

Table of Contents

CHAPTER 1

What You Will
Learn From This Book

Do you know how to trust your gut? What happens when you read that line? What do you feel? Is there a lightning second of surety and then a kaleidoscope of confusion and doubt and second-guessing? Or are you all in, totally dialed and self-assured? If you are like me, you may have the swirly, gooey mess of uncertainty in your gut because your natural instincts were bullied, hammered, and shamed out of you from a crappy childhood and ensuing trauma.

I know firsthand that living with trauma can feel like you are getting punched in the gut on repeat; it makes you breathless, buckles your knees, and convinces you to keep your guard up at all times. It can lead to a hyper-arousal state of hypervigilance, where you are constantly on guard for potential threats. This guarded state of being uses up considerable mental and emotional resources, making it difficult for intuitive signals to be heard or felt. It can also lead to a hypo-arousal state where you shut down, becoming totally immobilized or dissociative. In a shutdown state, it is also too difficult to listen to your gut instincts. This mode of being may be your default survival state, and you may not be conscious of it; you may think it is just your personality. Your survival states will have you reacting to cycles of emotional dysregulation.

In order to interrupt those cycles, you have to relearn what your body is saying. What are the messages in your tissues? What are those gut instincts telling you? How can you feel those messages if feeling into your body doesn't feel safe? This book will teach you how to hear the language of your nervous system so you will be able to discern what is a response to your trauma and what is your gut instinct.

Throughout this book, I will invite you to consider how people, places, and things have impacted you. I will teach you how trauma is a stored survival response that can originate from illness, being under anesthetics, and motor vehicle accidents. We'll also discuss what we call Big T and Little t trauma. I will strive to be sensitive in the presentation of this multi-directional toolkit, provided within these pages, that presents ways to heal and bring safety back into your body-mind. Body-mind is the holistic self; it is your brain, your body, your mind, your emotions, and your spirit. The whole self. Mind-body and body-mind will be used interchangeably.

Most people operate from a single point of awareness that is rooted in survival mode or a default survival state. Implementing multi-point awareness techniques will help you grow your capacity to move from survival mode into a safe, expanded mode of being. You are a beautiful, complicated, quantum being with your own unique history. If you do not safely enquire into the who, what, and how of the issues in your tissues, and then interrupt those patterns of behaviour from within, you will repeat sequences of reactivity that cause you problems.

Healing (interrupting patterns of dysregulation) requires repetition. I use repetitive language in this book to access your higher mind and to imprint new thought-stepping cycles. The more you are exposed to these principles, the more readily you will grasp and accept them. You will see the acronym PEMS throughout the book. This represents the physical, emotional, mental, and spiritual hygiene techniques that can expand your bandwidth for stress and stored survival responses. Hygiene typically means practices or conditions that are conducive to health. The word Hygiene ultimately comes from ancient Greek, hugieiné tekhné, meaning "the art of health," and when you think about it, any art requires practice. Practicing PEMS hygiene and the art of health is no different. Hygiene requires daily, consistent, repetitive, ritualistic focus. Think about your nighttime routine or getting ready for work. You have a hygiene routine to keep yourself clean, to keep your environment healthy, and to practice a preventative style of care to ensure optimal output.

The PEMS hygiene system is similar; it is there for you to establish your own unique code of ethics for healing and personal protection strategies. Learning PEMS hygiene gives you a routine to anchor yourself, steadying the mind-body for all that life continues to throw at you.

Multi-Systems Approach Using PEMS

- **Physical:** You need a physical routine. I am a huge advocate of somatic movement, yoga therapy, and intelligent jiu-jitsu, and I write about these practices the most in this book. Movement is essential for healing, as it dislodges the trapped survival energy in the body.

- **Emotional:** A continual wonderment for what you are feeling, when you feel it, and with whom you feel it is highly encouraged. Feeling your feelings is different than intellectualizing your feelings. Feeling is a body based felt sense. Not a thinking space. Feeling your feelings breeds emotional intelligence and reduces reactivity because you understand what your emotional baseline is and who, what, and how it gets activated. This state of activation can be considered a trigger. From the perspective of psychology, triggers are events that happen around us (and, less often, inside us) that cause us to have particular emotional reactions or behave in specific ways.[1] You are given many practices in this book to help you become reacquainted with feeling your emotional body and understand who, what, and when you get triggered.

- **Mental:** When you can understand that your brain wants to keep you comfortable, even if you are not safe, you will understand how to move outside of your comfort zone, safely. Physical education for the mind is called Psychoeducation. It encompasses the intellectual learning aspects of mental, emotional wellbeing and how to cope with illness. To intellectualize what you're thinking and feeling means understanding your nervous system blueprint and mapping your attunement to: safety, trust, power and control, intimacy, and self-esteem. When you hone your awareness to what you are thinking you develop Metacognition.

- **Spiritual:** Allowing you to invite a higher consciousness into your psyche. Use a term that resonates for you. This could be source energy, God, higher power, spirit, or animal guides. The main idea is accepting the concept that there is a higher knowing and that you are not alone. There is a source you can tap into. You will learn how to call back lost parts of yourself.

Fundamentally, your nervous system, your body, your personality, and your identity are a collection of energy: positive, negative, and neutral. From birth till this moment, you have exchanged energies with people, places, and things, which have, in turn, been an assortment of positive, negative, and neutral interactions, experiences, and events. Learning how to reclaim your energy is an important component of healing from the inside out. You get to learn these skills right away; no special equipment, location, or training partners are required.

---

[1] Miskewicz K; Fleeson W; Arnold EM; Law MK; Mneimne M; Furr RM; (2015). *A contingency-oriented approach to understanding borderline personality disorder: Situational triggers and symptoms.* Journal of personality disorders. https://pubmed.ncbi.nlm.nih.gov/26200848/

For now, I want to empower you with the awareness and knowledge that you can upgrade and re-organize your own nervous system operating system. When you read 'internal defense system' or 'default operating system,' I am referring to how you respond to life's stimuli. I want to introduce you to the basic five core needs that we need for healthy development. They are connection, attunement, trust, autonomy, and love/sexuality. If there was an interruption, violation, or denial of one of these core needs while you were developing, your nervous system will have registered this into its operating system. Your default operating system is essentially how your nervous system has learned to operate based on inputs from your birth until conscious re-arrangement. In the chapters on Your Nervous System Blueprint and Survival States, you will get even more clarity on how you have unconsciously built an internal defense system and default operating system based on your life experience.

For now, when you read those phrases, I want you to think about how your core needs were met while you were developing. How are your core needs for connection, attunement, trust, autonomy, and love/sexuality being met today? I want you to consider the contributing factors that influence how you respond to people, places, and things. This could be the first time you take a look at how you were raised and whether or not your core needs were fulfilled. This book is your invitation to consider how you developed certain behaviour patterns and thought processes. This can be an exploration into how experiences have accumulated in your operating system and what you can do to remove, heal, and repattern. You get to learn how to rewire your internal defence system so it stops playing the record of the past. You can start today, right now. Well, when you finish reading!

Please go gently, dear one, as you learn how to distinguish what is a trauma response and what is your intuition. Knowing the difference is how you can develop better personal protection strategies. Personal protection strategies help you develop a safety state of mind and create new patterns that support future growth and healing. Healing from trauma means you have a more measured, consistent output and is a result of cultivating awareness. Awareness means you can create space between emotions and actions. That space gives you the freedom to choose to either engage or disengage. This space that you can play with allows you to pause and observe the sensations in your body. Determining whether those sensations are from a memory bank that influenced your nervous system or if you're feeling in real time, what I call real-time processing. Cultivating this discernment is how you can find safety in your body-mind after living with trauma.

At first read, this may cause you to bristle, and I understand that your body may not feel like a safe space. I am here to help you find a degree of safety, a one degree shift even, so you can discharge the stored survival responses.

When you begin a new practice, your internal voice can be a brutal prosecutor, judge, and executioner. It can be a very convincing voice that sounds familiar, but that voice is usually bullshit.

It comes from years of having your own voice muted, betrayed, silenced, and shut down. We are all hardwired to give more weight or focus to things that go wrong than things that go right! This is the negativity bias, an overdeveloped survival mechanism that encourages you to pay attention to threats. Having a negativity bias means we habitually pay more attention to negative or bad energy exchanges. By giving them more attention, we make them more important than they really are, and this becomes our default setting until we learn to override it. To heal that inner prosecutor means you have to practice something called positive noticing. Without a teacher, therapist, guide, or coach, this is a tough journey. Let this book be your guide for now. You have to re-learn what it feels like to be positive. You need to notice the positive changes and even see the back slides positively. The negativity bias, coupled with the default programs, make you more comfortable with pain and suffering than the good things. This is okay, dear one, learning how to feel safe feeling good is a practice.

In most energetic exchanges or interactions with people, places, and things, we will:

- ▶▶ remember insults before we remember praises.
- ▶▶ recall big T or little T traumatic experiences better than positive experiences.
- ▶▶ ruminate about negative things more frequently than we think about positive things.

This is a mechanism of the negativity bias and why the negative inner voice is such a strong pattern. When something is hardwired in, it takes effort, focus, and desire to change. You will get many strategies here to rewire and repattern. Most significantly, you get to learn many ways to practice self-awareness, which teaches you how to name it to tame it. This repatterning and reorganization of thoughts, through feeling the feelings that those thoughts elicit, is how you override the negativity bias and buttress your PEMS hygiene system.

You also influence and reinforce the positive noticing circuitry when you learn how to override the negativity bias. Positive noticing is a skill that gets forgotten and overlooked. It takes practice to feel good after years of living in survival mode. It takes repetition to truly believe that you are worthy of feeling good but you can learn how to let the loudest voice in your head be the nicest! You will do this by rewiring your circuitry (your nervous system) and training yourself to be present using the information you will receive in this book. It is not your fault that your negative voice is so loud; your feelings are real, and your past is valid. Gaining the awareness to uncover the unconscious beliefs, thoughts, and emotions that are stored in your body-mind is how you create change. We do this by choosing new thoughts.

It may shock you to know that most humans are addicted to suffering.

It may shock you to know that most humans are addicted to suffering. They have created a feedback loop that creates a chemical addiction to striving for love and affection, for self-betrayal, and for burnout and despondency. This feedback loop will run automatically in the background, deceiving you into believing that these behaviours or people are safe because they are familiar. An addictive feedback loop is easy to depend upon because it is known to you. Suffering will feel comfortable until you make it conscious. Until you make it known to yourself how your autonomic nervous system is wired and what people, places, and things have an effect on you, you will still be operating in the unconscious. You may be comfortable, but you are not safe. Not in a way that supports your healing. You cannot distinguish what is trauma and what is intuition until you heal your nervous system, and your nervous system heals through feeling.

So, you will likely need to revisit sections of this book over and over again. As your capacity grows, your awareness will expand, and your ability to choose a different thought will develop. Learning how to repeat the process of interrupting thoughts and introducing a new pattern in your internal circuits and then, metaphorically, sitting with it, is how healing happens. Here's a saying you'll read a few times throughout this book:

> *Our minds can change our bodies.*
> *Our bodies can change our minds.*
> *Our behaviour changes the outcome.*

The brain is not in a fixed state as once believed. Neuroplasticity is the ability of the brain to form new connections and pathways and change how its circuits are wired. You can change the addiction to drama, suffering, and boundaryless living into safety. I want you to embrace the subtlety of this work, this practice. Subtle shifts and one-degree pivots are the goal.

One of the ways you'll make these shifts is by learning how to feel safe in liminal space, which I think of as "the space in between." It is the space you give yourself after reading a sentence and before moving on to a chore. Liminal space is non-doing. It is the time you take to simply be. I want you to take time, as you read, to introduce this liminal space into your routines. Even though I am giving you a multi-directional tool kit on how to develop your PEMS hygiene, please hear this: It is not just the collection of new information or the choosing of a new thought that creates change. This needs to be coupled with REST, non-doing in liminal space, and just feeling safe, to create the healing. The good news is that finding rest and safety is available to you again. Living in liminal space can become comfortable with practice and will supersede the former level of suffering. You get to reintroduce safety into your body-mind. You can also make these small shifts by learning how to discharge the stored survival responses and then sit with yourself and feel. We'll touch on this more later in the book.

Reintroducing safety takes time. You may already feel challenged by this strategy…perhaps thinking, "Who am I if I am not judging, critiquing, in pain, or suffering? That is my identity." It is okay if any of these thoughts cross your mind. It takes practice to think and feel different things. You get to create new habits that will stimulate the production of chemicals that support freedom and elevation in your internal defence system. Every time you have a thought, your body produces a chemical; you secrete a hormone.[2] You can do a quick mental catalogue right now on what thoughts you typically think and how you feel. Don't worry if you sense a pattern, that is the whole point. See your patterns and

---

[2] Dr. Joe Dispenza is a neuroscientist, lecturer, and educator who teaches how to rewire the brain and transform the body. This blog post titled *The thought of you*, published by Dr. Dispenza, June 10, 2019, is a great descriptor of the multi-layered chemical processes that occur by thinking a thought. https://drjoedispenza.com/dr-joes-blog/the-thought-of-you

influence change. If you need practice secreting the happy hormones, fear not; we all do. Human nature compels us to be comfortable, even if that comfort is not safe. Creating your PEMS hygiene system invites you to feel and think and think and feel. You are encouraged to learn how to be comfortable in the expanse, in the newness. This new place of thinking will become comfortable with practice, and it can become your new default pattern. This book will teach you how to rebuild your instincts for self-protection. Through implementing systems that you can repeat continuously, you can discover how to fulfil your needs: connection, attunement, trust, autonomy, and love/sexuality and reignite your capacity to hear your gut instincts.

The multi-directional toolkit within these pages involves these strategies:

- ▸▸ How to hone your intuition
- ▸▸ Identify your nervous system blueprint
- ▸▸ Recruit healthy boundaries
- ▸▸ Identify predator behaviour
- ▸▸ Rewire your internal survival state
- ▸▸ Cultivate situational awareness
- ▸▸ Stop self-abandoning
- ▸▸ Reclaim lost energy
- ▸▸ Interrupt the cycle of emotional dysregulation
- ▸▸ Fortify new coping mechanisms that re-orientate you back to safety and stabilization
- ▸▸ Expand your capacity to tolerate stressful situations
- ▸▸ Deliver undelivered communications to heal the stored survival stress or trauma in your body-mind
- ▸▸ Implement value-based actions to celebrate your progress
- ▸▸ Understand that self-protection is the ultimate self-care

▸▸ Learn how to avoid being gut punched

▸▸ Build a safety state of mind

Using the strategies in this book as a multi-directional resource and tool kit will support the changes required to find safety in a new level of comfort. But, I need to include a warning here, as being forewarned is being forearmed. Remembering hurtful, charged, negative, or traumatic events will bring with them emotions and feelings that could be overwhelming. When recalling something fearful or highly charged, the brain and your nervous system will respond just as if it is happening all over again. If you have Big T or Little t trauma, personal protection can feel intimidating, and healing can seem impossible. You may not know how to feel safe in your body. You may misread safety cues and red flags, mistaking a toxic bond for love and affection. You may have had a chronic illness or injury that has prohibited your body from feeling strong. I got you. Nowhere in this book are we going to go balls deep (intentional, punchy language) into reliving or unearthing the motherload of traumatic events. What I am going to do is show you how to recognize patterns of reactivity and behaviour, both within yourself and from the outside world of people, places, and things.

This book will also introduce you to the notion that healing means feeling more comfortable with the life you have lived to date. Part of this is healing so you can hear those gut instincts and trust yourself to create boundaries around your self-care. By the end of this book, you will succinctly connect to changing your physiology by relearning how to meet yourself in your own body. Self-awareness can become a habit just as suffering or attachment to chaos or drama can become a habit. Part of this new self awareness is learning how to do positive noticing, notice not just the bad things, but the good things as well. Notice your positive traits, accomplishments and things you do well in this world. Once you connect to the PEMS hygiene you can give yourself a break, cut yourself some slack and reintroduce safety as the ultimate self care routine. Cradle your new beginnings as you would a puppy, with absolute care, devotion, and unconditional love. Get ready and go easy! Allowing yourself to feel powerful may be a foreign concept. It takes time to become comfortable feeling powerful and in control. Safety may feel like a betrayal at first if you have been conditioned to find chaos familiar. Healing is not straightforward; you will gain traction with some of these techniques and then fall into familiar feedback loops. Don't give up. You are deserving and worth it, dear one, in every possible fucking way!

CHAPTER 2

Why I Wrote This Book

One of the main things I want to achieve with "Gut Punch" is to save you some time so that your healing and self-defence journey is smoother than mine was. I wrote this book to empower you to feel safe, capable, and confident enough to practice personal protection strategies because, for me, true, holistic healing is embedded in self-defence. They truly are one and the same. Healing means you can manage the stress of life without burnout. Personal protection means you know how to keep yourself safe from threats outside of yourself and from threats within yourself. To heal from a gut punch, you need to be able to sit in the aftermath and reintroduce safety. If you have sustained a series of traumatic events or experiences, you need to discover where your stored survival stress is being held in your body. This will reignite your gut instincts to read people, places, and things through a clear lens and not through the lens of a trauma response.

I grew up in a small mountain community in British Columbia, Canada. We were poor and lived on the wrong side of the tracks, literally, across from the Trans-Canada Highway in a dugout of a trailer park. My mom worked two jobs full-time, and my stepdad was a violent man with a raging temper. I had an older brother who was preoccupied and a younger brother whom we doted on and took under our wings.

Logging towns in the 1980s were gritty places. My family was typical lower class: stressed, impoverished, overworked, and running from their own family dysfunction. With few resources or tools for betterment, the adults tried to do their best with what they knew but failed miserably. I witnessed the men in my family beat the women. I saw the women make excuses for them. I saw how abuse changes a woman until they are a shadow of their former self, permanently defeated, defensive, and wounded. I saw the men acting badly, with zero recourse or accountability. I was sexually assaulted, neglected, beaten, and verbally abused repeatedly. Random, unprovoked, chaotic, and violent episodes were the norm in my family system. Learning how to read a room before entering it, listening at the door to gauge the emotional temperature, and walking on eggshells anytime I was around the abuser was exhausting and totally terrifying. I was constantly told what my place was and asked how I dared to try to be better than that designated place.

Being latchkey kids, we were left to fend for ourselves and had chores and responsibilities that would be unheard of today. For example, I rode into town on my bike at age eight, along the Trans-Canada Highway for two kilometres, over the train tracks to DJ's Paper place to buy my own school supplies. Never mind the cleaning, child minding, ironing, laundry, and self-governance that was expected. Generation X grew up in a different timeline. It was laden with incessant, sanctioned child abuse by routine alcoholics who chain-smoked and smacked you randomly if they didn't like the look on your face. That was a common procedure. The more insidious abuse was a horror show bonus in my family. Today, I have learned that in tandem with generational violence, generational healing exists too!

Growing up, there were many times I tried to protect my mom when she was getting a beating. Instead of being thanked, however, I was punished and told I was making things worse. This was super confusing at the time and contributed to my self-defence instincts being hammered out of me.

I knew what I witnessed and experienced was wrong. I knew I wanted a better life regardless of how often I was told I got what I deserved.

Here are a few of the other things that were the norm in my family growing up that led to my state of mind being anything but one of safety:

- ▶▶ No one talked about the abuse.

- ▶▶ Boundaries were never honoured.

- ▶▶ Emotions were shamed, ridiculed, and denied.

- ▶▶ No one talked about trauma, dysregulation, or anxiety.

- ▶▶ No one modelled how to practice self-defence.

Until I learned how to heal from the inside out, the trauma-infused feedback loop kept unsettling me. It made me punish, question, and blame myself for not getting better. I judged myself for years by the industry standards of neuro-normative behaviour outputs. But those standards never really worked for me. They may not work for you, either. It took me years to feel safe enough to admit to myself how messed up my childhood was. In my family, still to this day, it is seen as a sign of strength to suffer silently, self-abandon, and not complain.

There is a concept called Adverse Childhood Experiences (ACE). We'll cover this in more detail later, but for now, all you need to know is that a person's ACE score is based on the types of abuse and household trauma they experienced as a child. My ACE score is 10 out of 10. To find out YOUR ACE score, visit Dr. Sara Gottfried's site @ https://www.saragottfriedmd.com or https://traumadissociation.com/ace.

There was little to no PEMS hygiene in my family system, and my body logged sustained threats into my nervous system everywhere, all the time.

As a result of my trauma, I developed an autoimmune disease, was diagnosed with endometriosis at 16, and had major gastrointestinal issues (colitis and irritable bowel syndrome) that made me become vegetarian, then vegan for 13 years, before I eventually started eating Celiac-friendly.

I wasn't diagnosed with C-PTSD, or Complex Post Traumatic Stress Disorder, until my forties, due in part to the relatively new discovery of the disorder and the sneaky way in which C-PTSD presents itself. These factors, coupled with the nauseating ignorance and lack of funding that goes towards women's health, led to my diagnosis taking decades. The amount of gaslighting I have received from the medical community, like millions of women beside me, is unconscionable and greatly contributes to the collective trauma women suffer at the hands of an ill-informed, poorly funded medical community.

Following along with contemporary self-help manuals, I would make some progress, and then I would be hit by a level of inertia, confusion, self-loathing, and debilitating doubt because I would regress. I would think all progress was lost until I understood that most contemporary healing models do not adequately address or understand C-PTSD. I mean, come on…it is complex for a reason. It does not follow any rules and can have you floundering in a world that is only just getting up to speed about how it manifests. C-PTSD has become more prevalent due to the sustained, multi-factor traumatic episodes that people experience. Healing from C-PTSD requires a multi-systems approach for you to be successful in gaining more peace, less reactivity, and cultivating a safety state of mind.

I left home before I graduated high school. Mom had married husband number three by my senior year. He was a lecherous lout who was even worse than the last one, so staying home and navigating this new shit show was not an option. I went to Lake Louise, a resort town, and worked an early shift (6am–2pm). This left many hours to play in the mountains. I didn't know then that my dysregulated nervous system sought out adventure and stimuli because I was accustomed to danger. Rock climbing, cliff jumping, extreme mountain biking, and Alpine skiing were all my chosen outlets at the time to feed the adrenalized form of activity that I resonated with.

From there, I went to Calgary, Alberta, and worked at the Roasterie in Kensington. I met a friend who dreamed as big as me and introduced me to the Gulf Islands. It was on Galiano Island, BC, that I did yoga for the first time. I was 19, and it was the first time I felt like I could control how my body felt. I could influence healing and create states of well-being. This was a total game-changer for me! Experiencing safety for the first time in my body through yoga therapy allowed me to feel the anxiety and panic that was stuck in my body due to the violation of my core needs from my dysfunctional childhood. I also felt incredible rage after my yoga session. There would be peace and calm and relief from moving my body, but afterwards, I would be cagey, bitchy, dissatisfied…it was a slow creep that would take over within hours after practicing. For years, this rage would unveil itself in my tissues after doing yoga. Rage and anger were not safe emotions growing up. I had to reclaim these powerful emotions.

Rage and anger are natural byproducts of not having a need met or having a boundary disrespected. Honouring these emotions allowed me to move them out of my tissues. I give you some wonderful tools in this book so you can move the anger and rage out of your tissues, too. My healing journey has led me to doing shamanic ceremonies, holotropic breathwork, angel workshops, Gabriel Roth 5 Rhythm's dance, vipassana meditation, sweat lodges, family constellations, human design, Hakomi technique, and cold plunges. I offer this list as a declaration to you that I have been on this journey for over 30 years. I have come to my level of expertise through experiential learning, practical application, and decades of service in the craft of teaching wellness. I teach what works from what I know to be true. I want this book to offer you the very best distillation of my tried and true remedies and techniques.

I am certified in Ashtanga Yoga, Pre- & Postnatal Yoga, and Yoga Therapy. I am also a certified Shiatsu Practitioner, Meditation Teacher, and licensed BodyMind Coach. As of this writing I am a Blue Belt in Ribeiro Jiu-Jitsu, which is a Brazilian martial art (also called BJJ), and a 6th-degree Black Belt in KoKoDo JuJutsu, which is a Japanese martial art. In 2023 I earned the title of Menkyo Kaiden Shihan or 6th Dan, Licensed, Master Instructor with full transmission.

In 1999, I started training in jiu-jitsu, and I was profoundly shocked at how unnatural protecting myself felt. I had no idea I would stick with it for over 25 years and obtain the degree of Menkyo Kaiden Shihan, making me the first woman in North and South America to hold this title!! When I was starting out, my joints would willingly bend past the point of safety to comply with an arm lock, and I would experience a jumble of sensations that frequently overwhelmed me. Initially, I never knew I was being constantly triggered on the mat. I didn't realize that I was disassociating and fawning and/or freezing while learning jiu-jitsu, and I did not have the language for my behaviour for decades. I could just feel the people-pleasing/'minimize the damage' persona show up. Or, other times, it would be the 'shutdown and comply' persona. When I began jiu-jitsu, it was a long, tedious road of battling myself, overriding the default programming that showed up relentlessly. The default programming was that I didn't deserve protection.

Somatically, meaning in my felt-body-sense, my body did not respond the way I needed it to. Getting my right leg to bear weight while deflecting a punch was hard in the beginning. Subconsciously, my nervous system was being intensely activated in these simulated fight scenarios. I was not aware of why I would feel feelings or how or when those feelings would come up when I was training, but the issues in my tissues responded. The rage and anger would creep in after training, just like in yoga. I did not have a language for what I was experiencing, and I did not know that I kept perpetuating cycles of reactivity because my nervous system was dysregulated. I had to learn the language of nervous system regulation so I could identify what I was feeling when I got on the mat. Predominantly, I felt unsafe protecting myself.

Every one of us has a pre-installed operating system based on the people, places, and things (otherwise known as inputs) in our lives. For me, I had inputs from being around unstable adults, having my home uprooted countless times before the age of 9, dealing with debilitating health issues from age 16 onwards to suffering injuries from an intense motor vehicle accident. Becoming a mother to twins at 24 and juggling life and output, I did not understand the sneaky ways anxiety would show up, I would second guess myself and not know how to trust my instincts. Before I understood how the nervous system worked, I kept repeating patterns of dysregulation, because of those logged inputs, that were automatically activated by the mandatory level of output required to succeed at life. This operating system, which is called your autonomic nervous system (ANS), is preloaded with software programs that were made during your developmental stage, even before you could speak or understand language, and are still being updated today.

My default factory settings had me afraid to protect myself.

If you do not practice nervous system regulation, your operating system runs on the default factory settings. This means that until you learn how to intentionally create experiences to override those programs and heal the somatic stress in your body-mind, you will be stuck in a never-ending feedback loop of faulty alarm systems and chronic dysregulation like I was for decades.

My default factory settings had me afraid to protect myself. Rage and anger were emotions I had learned to fear greatly. When I felt those emotions in my body, I would get overwhelmed and shut down. I did not know how to articulate my fears or tell an instructor what I was feeling. I thought I was bad or broken somehow. I kept doing jiu-jitsu.

Why? Because I knew I needed to feel safe protecting myself. I needed to rewire my internal operating system.

When I was training for Kaiden, immense concentration was required. Gruelling workouts were imperative to break down and break through to this level, and I trained for three years with an elite group of men. Part of the initiation to this level was a breakdown of the ego and all that you know. This is challenging for most, but especially for someone who has C-PTSD and clings fast to her quirks and habits to be able to feel safe.

During one of my accelerator training sessions, the concepts that day were eluding me. My mind was scrambled from receiving the techniques, mitigating the pain, and trying to perform this particular waza[3]. I began to ask questions. I was unaware that I had reached my limit and was digging in. My questions were relentless and could've been perceived as disrespectful. This is how I mask my anxiety and C-PTSD: asking questions and moving into my MIND space, my thinking space. When my body has reached its input limit, I get overwhelmed and exhausted and detach from feeling my body by thinking more and becoming analytical. This highly-stimulated, overwhelmed state kicks me into dysregulation and I dissociate and look to my mind to protect me.

If you have either of these conditions, you may understand that this protective, backdoor exit strategy is always at the ready. And the thing is, it's useful…until it is not; until you need to be present and respond to the tasks happening in real time. My personality gets shuttled off, and a new persona drops in; a nervous Nelly runs the show and uses whatever stopgaps she feels savvy enough to employ. In this case, curt, abrasive questioning.

My teacher (and husband) was patient and indulged nervous Nelly (me) to a point. And then, because I can mask expertly, he became frustrated by my lack of reception. I don't blame him. This is a tricky business

---

[3] Waza is a technical set of skills you perform in training or a technique. Done with compliance with a training partner.

managing complex trauma in a dojo where we are simulating fight scenarios and needing to avail ourselves to the training. In this particular training session, I could see my training partners getting suspicious. I could feel them willing me to be quiet and suffer without complaint, as is tradition when you are learning this rank. They are not being unkind; they are good students who are learning how to accommodate a woman with my background into the Kaiden club.

After my training finished, I just felt hollow. I was terribly activated, in a shutdown, frozen state, feeling abandoned and triggered. The air felt cold in the room, and there was not a lot of eye contact between me and my training partners. This is where my shame and inner prosecutor had the reins on a runaway Mustang. I had to avail myself to the energetic reprimand due to my behaviour.

Distinguishing what are my personal feelings versus what is required of me in training is a difficult dance. Jiu-jitsu does not discriminate; it asks the same of everyone, regardless of their back story. You have to learn how to live in the suck; you have to be comfortable being uncomfortable. This is why training in jiu-jitsu is so valuable if you have C-PTSD or other forms of trauma. It is a uniform requirement to show up, train, succeed, fail, not take it personal, level up, and repeat. Over and over again. This training session was different only in the level of skill I was being asked to perform. It was not a personal attack. The attack came from myself, from within me and my dysregulation. I had to stop the violence within. The violence of a faulty operating system that attacked itself through dysregulated behaviours.

Unhealed childhood trauma will erect an internal prosecutor that is Judge Judy on steroids. Not to be confused with an internal critic because critics can be useful. A critic can be consulted to decide on a restaurant or a movie to watch. The voice of this internal prosecutor is not a nice voice! It will tell you that you are not good enough, too needy, weak, and incapable. The voice tells you lies and wants you to forget who you really are: a beautiful, bio-electrical, quantum being worthy of love and goodness!

Dr. Glenn Doyle,[4] licensed psychologist, has this to say about the inner prosecutor:

> *"The more trauma you've endured, the more committed…*
> *the internal prosecutor is—and the more creative and devious*
> *he is in his arguments…He often speaks in language*
> *and tone that we recognize from way back when.*
> *His arguments often sound "right" because they are familiar.*
> *Sometimes he's been in our ear for decades, "winning" case*
> *after case by making us feel like sh*t about ourselves."*

Having the internal prosecutor run wild in your unconscious is violence towards yourself. The internal prosecutor is a mechanism of your psyche, fed from the negativity bias, nourished by unmet core needs, and fortified through self-limiting beliefs. The negativity bias is a survival mechanism that encourages you to pay attention to threats. What was initially a good mechanism becomes an overdeveloped switch that has you more susceptible to heavy, consistent criticism making that negativity bias much more prominent and hard to distinguish.

Have you ever had a hard time pinpointing what you are feeling after a movement class or body session? When you don't feel good or bad; you just feel worked? Well I did, and when I wanted to understand what the issues in my tissues were trying to communicate, I came up with the term somatic sludge. Somatic sludge is what I coined to describe the heavy, pervasive, wild, unpredictable pattern of sensations that my body would share with me after class. That cagey, bitchy feeling I had been experiencing for years needed a definition. I realized that for decades, I

---

[4] Cited from Dr. Glenn Doyle, a licensed psychologist, director of The Doyle Practice, and author of the blog, *Use Your Damn Skills*. September 7, 2023 Blog entry titled, The internal prosecutor and trauma recovery.

had had this somatic sludge show up after yoga therapy and jiu-jitsu. It describes the way my body would release her alarms and trapped survival responses; in essence, the trauma stored in my tissues (in my body). Somatic sludge is my delicious new term for when you feel movement and change but cannot articulate the emotion or feeling because it is ALL the emotions and feelings pulsing through you.

We all need to know how to live with somatic sludge. It gives context to the 'issues in your tissues.' It allows the body to be heard in multi-faceted awareness—all the sensations that are stored in your cells, in your muscles, in your skin. By feeling into your somatic sludge, you will relearn how to feel safe in your body. You will rewire the inputs so they know your body is allowed to change, emit, transmute, and feel. To heal your nervous system, you have to become comfortable with feeling into the body. You cannot think yourself into healing. You have to feel your way through it, which is hard. Very, very hard. But so very, very worth it.

I wrote this book to help you identify what your default patterns are so you can interrupt them and fortify a new self-protective state of being! The multi-systems approach and accompanying strategies are all designed to re-pattern and re-program your default operating system.

Interrupting my default programming from childhood and my life lived to date is how I learned to heal my trauma and cultivate a safety state of mind. Healing does not mean I am calm and non-reactive. Healing means that I am curious, engaged, present, and able to handle the stress of life without it overwhelming me to the point of isolation. Lexi Florentina holds a masters in Psychology and is a trauma trained somatic experiencing practitioner on a mission, just like mine, to support humans to return to safety in their body. This is her quote:

"The opposite of trauma isn't to find perfection,
to become a contained or even calm version of ourselves.
But rather, it's where we begin to experience what
couldn't exist when all our body could do was survive."

I wrote this book to teach you how to restore your gut instincts so you can listen and act from intuition instead of a stored survival response. Healing the issues in your tissues takes time, so please, be kind to yourself as you learn these strategies.

CHAPTER 3

Self Defence as a Mindset

Traditionally, self-defence books show a bunch of techniques on paper. Techniques that are difficult to replicate without an in-person instructor and dedicated training times. You get to see groin shots, throat punches, choke holds, and strikes. These books never mention the emotions that you have to deal with to execute these dynamic defences, outside of anger or rage. Not to mention, those defenses are an unrealistic response for someone with no training.

This is not a manual of physical techniques. I encourage you to seek out a qualified instructor[5] for on-the-mat training to learn how to physically thwart an attacker.

Nor is this purely a self-help empowerment book. Those books focus on the repetition of affirmations, positive self-talk, and a self-care routine so you can manifest to your heart's delight. They do not teach you that your intuition may be stunted as a result of your trauma or that finding the motivation to do self-care practices will wax and wane quicker than the moon. Rarely do they go into teaching you what state your nervous

---

[5] Visit my website www.sadohana.com for training options and to reach out to me for suggestions on training in your area. I am happy to help you vet potential instructors or self-defence programs.

system is in or how to understand the alarm system in your body. The alarm systems that result in not being able to cope with the world around you and the ensuing pervasive anxiety, insomnia, and feeling triggered by everyday commitments.

They also often neglect the nuances needed for someone who has a chronic illness or a disability. They rarely address neurodivergent individuals. Individuals like myself, whose brains develop or work differently. Neurodivergent people have different strengths and weaknesses from those whose brains work more typically. We simply do not process information the same way as neurotypical people. I tried for years to use a positive mindset to quell my anxiety to no avail.

You need to have a body-based practice with cognitive behavioural therapy to heal anxiety. Something like yoga therapy, somatic movement, somatic therapy, or trauma-informed jiu-jitsu, accompanied by talk therapy sessions. Mindset work caters to the neurotypical—individuals whose brains process information and read social cues 'normally.'

Most mindset work is an external, output, achievement mode with little allowance for the complicated survival style of someone who has suffered from trauma and processes differently. Maybe you never think about your nervous system outside the fact that you have a brain and nerves. That is okay, dear heart! This book is here to re-introduce a new level of safety within your own body. Showing you that self-defence is a mindset and telling you that you have just as many nerve cells in your gut (enteric nervous system) as you do in your spinal cord is the up-leveling, thought-stepping exercise that will help you move out of survival mode.

When you move out of survival mode, your ability to hear your gut instincts telling you a known associate is dangerous for you comes back online. From my decades of teaching humans and being in the martial arts and yoga communities, I know there is a lot of janky information out there when it comes to self-defence and healing. My main issues are that they perpetuate the myth that self-defence is about fighting and healing is about doing! In the subsequent chapters, we focus on the ways to sit with a practice for healing, so for now, let's focus on learning why most self-defence teachings are inadequate.

Here are four specifics I want to highlight:

1 | It is careless to teach severe, injurious techniques without educating on the justifiable use of force.

2 | Not everyone can possess the amount of violence within them to execute such a vicious attack. I mean, most people have a hard time speaking up when they feel like their boundaries have been trespassed, let alone having the presence of mind to angle their thumb just so and apply just the right amount of pressure into someone's eyeball.

3 | Physical confrontations should be taught as a last resort because they are dangerous and require a commitment and follow-through that most casual participants will not have.

4 | Without taking care of the nervous system and the feeling aspect of self-defence, there is a risk of re-traumatizing yourself.

Let's be realistic: unless you are training in a reality-based martial arts program two to three times a week, fighting is not something you should consider. Your best self-defence technique is going to be using your Attitude, Awareness, and Avoidance; the three A's! These are the three foundational pillars for self defence/self-care. We get into the nitty-gritty in the ensuing chapters. Briefly, awareness is the skill of being tuned into yourself and the world at large; avoidance teaches you to avoid people, places, and things that put you in harm's way; and having an attitude of confidence can dissuade potential attackers and energy vampires in your life.

The principles in this book are designed to teach you how to recreate safety within. So you can hear what your gut is saying based on real-time processing and not a faulty feedback loop from the past. Faulty feedback loops disrupt cognitive functioning, decision-making, and the ability to experience joy.

It is important to state that there are no silver bullets when it comes to self-defence. For every scenario you can think of, there are a multitude of counterattacks. This book cannot teach you every counter to every attack! No self-defence training can do that, and if a school or instructor tells you they can teach you "all the self-defence techniques you will ever need to know" in a class or workshop, understand this is a slick marketing schtick and not a realistic or trustworthy source.

Using self-defence as a personal care strategy recognizes that you are a dynamic, bioelectrical, quantum being that needs tools to develop a whole body system of physical, emotional, mental, and spiritual hygiene techniques. These personal protection strategies will expand your bandwidth for stress and difficult inputs so you can be safe inside and out! I will show you how to recognize patterns of behaviour that have become a habit and encourage you to discern whether or not those patterns and habits are useful.

What is the safest thing to do?

Self-defence is not just a physical practice, and it is not just about fighting. Returning you to safety is my number one concern. From now on, I want you to always ask yourself, "What is the safest thing to do?" Let that be your guiding principle as you embark on your Gut Punch journey and learn how to heal from the inside out.

Self-defence is a natural, innate instinct, and when you know better, you do better. When you understand how past events will influence present and future outcomes, you are more prepared to handle stressful inputs.

This is why I am a huge advocate for nervous system regulation and reclaiming lost energy as a self-defence strategy. When you can distinguish the real threats from the alarm states within your body, your perception of what happens outside of your body expands and improves greatly.

Having taught thousands of women self-defence, I have witnessed that most people are not in touch with their nervous systems. Most people do not know the difference between combatives and self-defence. In my classes, I see them morph from meek, passive, shutdown behaviour to hyper-aggressive and bombastic behaviour. They lack self-control when we start to learn strikes and ground positions. Their voices go slack when I ask them to state a boundary and maintain a confident stance.

This is totally normal because:

1. It is extremely uncomfortable to anticipate potential violence.

2. It is very scary to vocalize a need if you have a history of not having needs met.

3. It feels unpredictable when your body learns new movement inputs.

4. When you are met with resistance, it feels like a threat.

The punch line here is most people feel uneasy protecting themselves. Especially women.

Most people feel uneasy protecting themselves. Especially women.

In a self-defence scenario where you are being confronted with a potential predator, being assertive rather than aggressive is important. Being assertive gives the potential attacker a way out, so to speak. They will not feel like they have to defend their position, or their potential position, by reacting. Their ego doesn't get damaged, and they do not perceive a sense of loss. You want to give them a way out—this is avoiding potentiality.

Most predators or bullies are cowards, and if they feel challenged or disrespected, they can behave badly. You want to give them a chance to behave well. This is strategy. Being assertive is a respectful way to maintain your boundaries without inflaming a situation. Being assertive and not aggressive is very important because being aggressive towards a potential attacker can make them want to respond out of pride and defensiveness. This strategy is to keep you safe by understanding their tactics and their weaknesses.

Learning to communicate assertively is also how you can state a boundary and communicate how you wish to be treated and dealt with. It is important to state that it is not your job to prevent an assault or an attack. Prevention implies you have a choice to act a certain way. The only person who can prevent an assault is the attacker or perpetrator. You are learning self-defence because violence is a reality, not your responsibility. It is important that you understand the strategies laid out in this book are to fortify your internal defence system (nervous system) and cultivate your safety state of mind. Always be aware it is NEVER your responsibility to prevent bad people from behaving badly or your fault when they do so!

Knowing how to communicate is a skill in and of itself. We all want to be assertive, confident, respectful, and non-threatening, yet we don't always succeed. Depending on the people, places, and things you encounter, your communication style may waiver and change. Typically, you will employ a variation of the three most common communication styles: passive, aggressive, and assertive. Passive communicators typically avoid confrontation and may struggle to express their opinions or needs openly. Aggressive communicators can be pushy and dominant and ignore others' viewpoints or opinions. Assertive communicators are able to convey thoughts, feelings, and opinions without disrespecting other people. This communication style is direct and self-assured without resorting to aggression or passivity.

Being able to hear another point of view, even if you do not agree with it, without reacting in a hostile, snarky, or dismissive manner is assertive communication. Learn how to use an assertive communication style. This will give you a baseline of what to expect in others and when to notice if that baseline shifts. You will be able to detect when someone switches to aggressive communication or passivity as a ploy. Don't worry, by the end of this book, you will have read and learned many ways to build assertive muscles.

Let me ask you:

1. Can you tell if someone is grooming you for future advantage?

2. Do you know what predatory behaviour is?

3. What is a healthy boundary?

4. Would you know how to identify a threat cue?

5. Do you prepare exit strategies?

6. Can you trust your gut?

7. How does stress show up in your life?

8. What beliefs have you inherited from your family system?

Really take a moment and think about those questions. There are no right or wrong answers to them. They exist to invite your mind into the type of emotional and spiritual baggage you carry, as well as to elicit healthy communication strategies within yourself so you can live safely in this world. Self-defence teaches you how to mitigate the harm done by predators AND low-functioning people.

We all have PEMS baggage; it is the gift of being human. Learning self-defence will help you heal so that you can determine what is a trauma response and what is your intuition. It is an excavation and organization of your personal PEMS hygiene routine, so it works for you rather than hinders you.

The practices in this book will help you re-frame your anxiety by understanding the alarm system in the body. When you understand when or why your alarm system fires off, you can heal the issues in your tissues, which enables you to exist with people, places, and things from a more balanced, holistic state. An alarm in the body can come from past events, like a medical intervention, a motor vehicle accident, or chronic illness. When you understand how readily your body will store a survival response or experience a trapped alarm, you are on your way to clearing the issues in your tissues. You can more readily recognize threats around you when your nervous system experiences states of feeling regulated. By learning how to recognize behaviour patterns both in yourself and in others, you will be able to identify danger and threat cues, increasing the likelihood of avoiding inputs that can cause you harm.

Under Canadian law, self-defence provides people with the right to protect themselves if attacked or under threat of attack. It is also the protection of one's person or property against some injury attempted by another. When discussing the physical application of self-defence it is imperative to understand what is called 'justifiable use of force.'

What does that mean? Well, if someone physically uses self-defence, they must be able to articulate why they did what they did based on the attack and perceived threat they were under. They must be able to justify 'reasonable use of force.' Reasonable use of force is justifiable when it appears reasonably necessary to prevent an impending injury. There is a distinction between non-deadly force and deadly force. This is literally how it sounds: A non-deadly force can be used to repel a non-deadly attack or a deadly attack, however, deadly force is justifiable if used to fend off a deadly attack but not justifiable if the attacker is NOT using deadly force.

Okay, take a breath, and let's unpack that a bit. If someone pushes you and then starts to walk away, and you grab a baseball bat and smash in their face, this would be considered non-justifiable deadly force because you weren't facing someone using deadly force. But what does deadly force look like? Well, if you are being pinned to the ground and an attacker is on top of you, holding a weapon, that could be considered deadly use of force. Multiple attackers, choking, repeated heavy blows, and force that causes grievous bodily harm can all be examples of deadly force.

What is an assault?[6]

Assault

265 (1) A person commits an assault when

(a) without the consent of another person, he applies force intentionally to that other person, directly or indirectly;

(b) he attempts or threatens, by an act or a gesture, to apply force to another person, if he has, or causes that other person to believe on reasonable grounds that he has, present ability to effect his purpose; or

(c) while openly wearing or carrying a weapon or an imitation thereof, he accosts or impedes another person or begs.

Here are some questions you can ask yourself to help you determine if you are in imminent danger of being assaulted:

- ▶▶ Does the assailant have or appear to have the ability to behave as you perceived?

- ▶▶ Does the assailant demonstrate intent?

- ▶▶ Do words and actions or body language lead you to believe the assailant has the intent to attack you?

- ▶▶ Does the assailant have the means to attack you?

---

[6] Government of Canada, https://laws-lois.justice.gc.ca/eng/acts/c-46/section-265.html

Again, take a deep breath. I know it can be activating reading about bodily harm and the use of force. It is never my intention to scare you. I want to arm you with as much knowledge as this book allows so you can practice with physical, emotional, and mental intelligence. These are the broad strokes you need to know to employ effective personal protection strategies. The chapters on Threat Cues, Predatory Behaviour, Situational Awareness, and Healthy Boundaries will illuminate in more detail techniques you can employ for safety.

Self-defence does not mean fighting; self-defence is a state of mind.

Now that you have a bearing on the legality of self-defence, let's get back to the beautiful nuance of personal protection techniques and how you can hone them to suit your needs. This book is teaching you many ways to cultivate a safety state of mind, in tandem with taking care of the emotional cargo that you show up with. Trauma is the result of not feeling safe and having had injurious events happen to you. Trauma interferes with being able to listen to your gut so it is imperative to invite new strategies into your personal care routine and PEMS hygiene system to bring awareness into all the magnificent ways you are you. I call this self-defence from the inside out because you are learning how you are wired on the inside and what is stored in your nervous system, which is your internal defence system. Here, self-defence is synonymous with self-care. Self-defence does not mean fighting; self-defence is a state of mind.

My own healing journey is deeply informed by the practices I do, primarily somatic yoga therapy and jiu-jitsu. Don't worry if your mind is grappling with how that makes sense; by the end of this book, you will have a greater understanding. I simply bring this up to anchor your awareness in this new philosophy of how personal protection is self-care and self-care is having good personal protection strategies.

Now, while they are linked, your internal defence system is not the same as self-defence. One is your nervous system, and the other is a deliberate sequence of thoughts and behaviours used to keep you safe and influence your nervous system patterning. Here's a saying I really like:

"Nerves that fire together wire together."

You get to make the mind and body work together, and if you do it once, you can do it again. A one-degree shift, a slightly different thought, a slightly different action; these are your goals. Once you learn how your default autonomic nervous system has organized itself, you can influence change and reorganize your nervous system so it is a path for your future instead of a record of the past, allowing you to hear your gut instincts over your trauma. This is self-defence.

I want to help you understand that when you begin to implement personal protection strategies and deploy self-defence systems, you will trigger your autonomic nervous system. You have inputs that are stored in your ANS that get triggered when you begin to step out of your comfort zone and try new behaviours. For example, when you start to play with healthy boundaries, it will feel difficult. If you have had your core needs chronically denied in the past, trying something new will feel very foreign and, initially, will cause anxiety. Keep going! Doing something that is healthy and empowering can feel dangerous if you have a faulty alarm system. In all likelihood, you have never been able to prioritize your safety and wellbeing, until now.

Please go easy with yourself as you learn these new skills. It takes time to rebuild confidence in your instinct for self-protection. It takes time to heal trauma and feel safe claiming your power and space in the world. Healing is non-linear, and learning how to reconnect with your body takes time when there has been a baseline of feeling unsafe. This reconnection to your body and to your environment, with safety as your goal, will be subtle and nuanced. As your range of resilience expands, you will be able to tolerate people, places, and things with less likelihood of emotional dysregulation. This PEMS hygiene toolkit is to bolster your confidence in being able to reintroduce safety in your body.

CHAPTER 4

Gut Punch—Intuition

A gut punch can be a literal, hard hit to your stomach. The gut punch I refer to in this chapter, and throughout this book, is a figurative blow to your PEMS system. It is something that hurts or damages you emotionally, mentally, or spiritually. And it can feel physical because it is such a shock and disturbance that it evokes a visceral feeling.

A gut punch is a sudden, devastating emotional blow. It can be a betrayal or an emotional disruption to your internal operating system, usually perpetrated by someone in a position of trust in your life. Being exploited, intentionally deceived, or unexpectedly disappointed can feel like a gut punch. This emotional disturbance is akin to having the wind taken out of your sails.

A gut punch is a sudden, devastating emotional blow.

A gut punch is different from a gut instinct. The latter infers intuition, a figurative, inner voice that serves to protect you. A gut punch is wounding. A gut instinct is self-protection. Learning how to heal one so you can hear the other is what this chapter is about.

A great example of a figurative blow or gut punch between 2 people, can be seen in an episode of Downtown Abbey, a fabulous television series created by Julian Fellowes. In Season 6, episode 8 of the series, the character, Lady Mary is intensely dysregulated and self sabotaging and she lashes out with a verbal wounding to her father, Lord Grantham. In this scene she delivers the line, "Do you still think dismissing Barrow was a useful saving?" Visibly shocked by this unexpected, hurtful gut punch from his daughter, he replies, "That's rather below the belt, even for you." The character Lady Mary intended to wound and land a punch to the gut with her question. Can you identify when someone has used a figurative gut punch on you?

What I didn't know until much later in my healing journey, and want to save you time in accessing, is that if you have sustained a series of gut punches, listening to your gut becomes impaired. Trauma changes how your intuition perceives the world around you and how you behave in it. This is important to know because you may have developed a habit of self-blame, criticizing yourself for not responding to red flags or gut instincts, not realizing that your internal radar has been impaired. Trusting your intuition becomes corrupted when you have been mistreated. The best news is that you can restore it.

Intuition, or a gut instinct, is the ability to know something without conscious reasoning. I use intuition and gut instinct interchangeably; they are the same. You are born with a gut knowing, a gut instinct. You are born with an innate intuitive sense. Intuition is being able to interpret the nuanced emotional associations you have with a person, place, or thing while deciphering your learned patterns and accessing a higher knowing. The higher knowing that exists without conscious reasoning.

As stated above, sustaining a series of gut punches can wound or corrupt your intuition. Your gut instincts can also become dulled by:

- ▸ Wounded core needs

- ▸ Trauma

- ▸ Abuse

- ▸ Unintentional neglect

- ▸ Intentional neglect

- ▸ Abandonment

- ▸ Societal conditioning

Trauma and intuition come from the same part of the brain, as do art and wisdom. The tricky part is summoning the correct response for the right occasion. Trauma and intuition reside deep in your psyche. Psyche refers to the totality of elements that form the mind, including conscious and unconscious experiences, personality, intellect, and the concept of the soul.

As mentioned, intuition is beyond conscious reasoning; it is the inner knowing that we are originally born with. When someone has been abused, conditioned to put others first (even at the expense of their own wellbeing), neglected, emotionally abandoned, and/or attacked, that inner knowing becomes eroded. The erosion is on par with your trust **Intuition is a skill that can be re-learned, re-awakened, and rekindled.** in people, places, and things. When trust is compromised, relying on one's own gut instincts becomes difficult. Due to the confluence of time and experience, you may have had a sustained impact on your nervous system—the internal defence system that informs your intuition. I do not want you to fret or worry if this is true for you. *Intuition is a skill that can be re-learned, re-awakened, and rekindled.*

Learning gut instincts is an action that builds upon itself, meaning once you start to do this practice, it is like making a deposit that will accrue interest with every effort you put in. The more you do it, the better you get. For many of you, this skill may be brand new. You may have had your gut instincts hammered down so relentlessly that you have to start from scratch. Learning how to decipher your gut instincts goes hand in hand with regulating your nervous system. Being able to interpret the emotional associations you have with a particular input will become more and more nuanced. You will begin to understand what is logged into your default operating system and how to override it. If you grew up in chaos, your nervous system registers chaos as familiar and safe. What may read as butterflies in your gut can, in actuality, be a reaction to an unsafe person, place, or thing. So what you originally intuit as butterflies and something fun and exciting may well be a trapped alarm, signalling danger. But you cannot interpret it as such until you learn what your default patterns are.

Regulating your nervous system is key to harnessing your gut instincts and listening to your intuition. You need to learn how to discern between fear, anxiety, a stored survival response, emotional memory, and the wisdom of your intuition. Deciphering a learned pattern is understanding what inputs your nervous system registered in utero, as a child, young adult, and adult. Those inputs for satisfaction or dissatisfaction, due to your core needs either being met or not being met, influence your internal defence system. It is completely normal (because collectively, as a society and in our unique family systems, it is very rare to have a good PEMS hygiene system) to need to re-learn, re-form and re-pattern your internal defence system and re-establish your intuition. Your nervous system has organized itself through your primary interpersonal relationships and having trust, love, connection, autonomy, and attunement with one another. Your nervous system will develop alarms and new organizational structures as you continue to experience new (or even old) inputs. You can change your body. You can change your mind. Your behaviour will change as a result.

Learning how to trust your gut will get easier when you take the time to be in your body and feel your feelings. I understand that being in the body can feel unsafe if you have big T trauma. It is my hope you have people around you who can support this skill-building, whether they be therapists, trusted family members, friends, or colleagues. If you do not have a support system, go gently. Feel free to skip around the book and visit other chapters. Just know that if you have sustained a gut punch to your internal defence system and have to start from scratch, there is hope. You can re-introduce safety into your feeling body. Be kind to yourself because we don't always get it on the first try. Be kind to yourself because you are practicing something new and you are allowed to not be good at it AND not give up. Keep going.

You can re-introduce safety into your feeling body.

Every moment of every day, your body is giving you feedback. Unfortunately, we are often taught to ignore our body's feedback through conditioning or convenience. Think about having to ask to go to the bathroom in grade school and being told to wait or not wanting to hug a certain uncle and being forced to. Women, in general, have been conditioned with 'nice girl' programming[7] and to put everyone else's needs first, becoming so attuned to others that they forget how to even hear the messages from within. This nice girl programming is pervasive, regardless of your culture. This program teaches women to go along to get along, be non-controversial, be chaste, be good, be above suspicion and reproach, be gentle, and that boys will be boys. This cultural conditioning mutes the ability to respond to intuitive hits and gut instincts.

Feeling safe in your body requires you to practice self-defence from the inside out. We'll touch on this more in the chapter on self-defence, but just know that I want to empower you to relearn what your gut

---

[7] Milton Rokeach, a Polish American social psychologist coined this phrase. The concept 'nice girl' is both an instrumental and terminal value: both a standard for and goal for behaviour. *"Persuasion that Persists"* Psychology Today 5 (September 1971): 68-71

instincts are so you can avoid being Gut Punched! Re-learning how to be aware of the feelings and sensations in your body is the first step in re-establishing the skill of intuition. It takes practice to listen to your body and the subtle messages it wants to deliver. But through simple, repetitive practices (outlined in this book), you can develop emotional hygiene and build your entire PEMS hygiene system.

PEMS hygiene will recondition your default patterns and internal defence system, literally changing the neural pathways and synapses to respond to need, demand, and fulfillment. This is how you can re-hone your gut instincts. To build your intuition, you need to interrupt the negative patterns that are a culmination of past and present experiences. Those unconscious patterns created a feedback loop that comprises your nervous system. The data inputs you collect throughout your life are programmed into your cells, which inform how you respond to people, places, and things. Recognizing when, what, and how you experience this feedback loop and bringing it from the unconscious to the conscious is what learning how to regulate your nervous system is all about.

This is also how you build the skill of listening to your gut instincts. It's about training yourself to be aware of how you feel, why you feel the way you do, and what makes you feel those feelings. Then, you consciously choose a different outcome to repattern your internal defence system. I will show you the reactivity feedback loop in more detail in the Survival Response chapter and you will get clearer on your default operating system in Your Nervous System Blueprint chapter, so don't worry if you're struggling to get your head around these concepts. Ideally, your nervous system becomes a solid defence system that protects you, as opposed to having an internal defence system that you are trying to recover from.

Here is an example of how a stored memory that was traumatic, initially confused my gut instincts. There was a boy who lived in my trailer park who terrorized me for years. He would chide me, embarrass me, chase me with gardener snakes, and assault me when I was young. My experiences with him left me with fear, trauma, and trapped survival responses (anxiety). If I meet someone who shares his name, I still get a gut hit to my nervous system that registers as apprehension, a tightening, and a wary withholding. This gut punch could be misinterpreted as intuition.

Looking at the situation in context, it is easy to see that this is not intuition; it is a gut response to the fear and trauma that he caused. Meeting new people that share his name provokes my internal defence system to recall the emotions and experiences that I had in the past. This abusive experience is a stored memory in the cells of my body that, upon hearing his name, responds to the past pain and influences the present moment. This particular trauma with this individual has caused significant stored survival responses within me that run automatically throughout my unconscious. Healing my nervous system by bringing to light the trauma that he caused allowed me to accurately view the damage to my internal defence structure. By following this 'name it to tame it' process, I was able to release this particular trauma associated with his name.

By healing my trauma (stored survival responses) bit by bit, I can now discern between genuine intuitive guidance and perceived threats. You, too, can learn the difference between an emotional memory, a stored survival response, and the wisdom of your intuition. Also, it is important to state that you do not need to relive every past trauma or buried emotion to heal. I do not believe that is necessary and it can even be harmful in certain instances. Talk therapy is rife with going over pain points and past experiences and, in most cases, only serves to retraumatize an individual. The multi-systems approach outlined here is not that. So take care, dear heart. You are safe here.

Listening to Your Gut is a Practice

Learning how to discern what energy you're feeling is a skill. A skill that must be practiced so you can remove the triggers of past experiences and fully integrate the present. A dysregulated nervous system, or an out-of-whack emotional hygiene system, uses up considerable PEMS resources, making it difficult for intuitive signals to be heard or felt.

Awareness of your triggers (people, places, and things that activate you in a negative way), your glimmers[8] (the opposite of a trigger, a glimmer is a person, place, or thing that brings you back to safety, joy, and calmness), your thoughts, your behaviour, your energy, and how you respond to positive and negative inputs is how you build your intuition. Tuning into your awareness allows you to hear the whispers of caution, your Spidey-sense, and feel the prickly sensation on your skin. Being attuned to these subtle changes helps you tap into a deep knowing that that belies conscious thought. This is how you decipher the gut instincts: by disentangling the emotional memories and reorganizing the unconscious patterns in your internal defence structure. It's about learning to differentiate what was then from what is now, living in the present, and healing trauma so you can interface in real time without the substantial baggage from your timeline.

How to Improve Your Intuition

You can improve your intuition by becoming aware of the feelings and sensations in your body. This is the first step to re-learning the skill of intuition. Every moment of every day, your body is giving you feedback. That feedback melds into the already established feedback loop that comprises your nervous system. Do you know how to feel the feelings? Can you sense a sensation in your body?

Intuition can be sensed in many ways. That uneasy feeling in your belly when you meet someone new who says all the right things but still makes you uncomfortable? This can be your intuition, picking up energy that

---

[8] Deb Dana, a Licensed Clinical Social Worker, (LCSW) consultant, author, and international lecturer coined the term "glimmers" in her book *The Polyvagal Theory in Therapy: Engaging the Rhythm of Regulation*. Published by W.W. Norton & Company, 2018

the mind has yet to decode. With good self-awareness, you can learn how to trust your intuition.

Having a thought leap into your mind that says, "Do not get a ride home with this person," even though you all have the same friends, coworkers, and colleagues, is your intuition sensing an intention that your reason didn't see.

With good self-awareness, you can learn how to trust your intuition.

Please understand that you never have to justify yourself when your awareness or intuition gives you a signal. You owe nobody an explanation. Listening to your internal guidance system will develop a deep sense of self-trust, which will grow and grow the more you use it. Listening to your gut instincts becomes money in the PEMS bank that grows every day.

Here are some tips that will help you improve your intuition:

Tip #1 Keep a journal

A dedicated Intuition Journal will help you untangle whether you are feeling a stored survival response, an emotion, or getting an intuitive gut punch.

The journal prompts are:

- ▸▸ What is this sensation or emotion? Example: I feel scared, I feel excited, I feel thirsty, I feel tired.
- ▸▸ Where in my body do I feel this? Example: in my chest, my toes are tingly, my brain feels heavy, the back of my head feels like cold water is running.
- ▸▸ What prompted this feeling, sensation or emotion? Example: the new guy at work asked me to stay late, my friend wants us to go away for the weekend, my mom wants me to plan her sister's party.

▶▶ Did I listen to my body? Example: I got cold shivers at the thought of going away, so I declined the offer.

▶▶ What was the outcome of me listening to my body? Example: there was a storm that closed down the highway, and the trip was cancelled.

▶▶ Was this an emotional charge, or was this intuition? Example: it was both, I had a sense not to go on the trip, and it got cancelled due to a natural disaster, protecting me from problem-solving on the fly or being caught in a predicament on the road.

The more accurate and honest you can be with yourself, the more revealing your journal exercises will be. Do not try to be right or get it right...allow yourself to rediscover for yourself what you feel, think, and feel!

Tip #2 Play a guessing game with yourself every week

For example:

▶▶ I wonder what colour the next car will be? Let me guess blue. Notice what the colour of the next car is and do it a few more times. Try to sense what colour the car that you've parked beside is.

▶▶ I wonder who will make eye contact with me in the store? Try to sense whether someone is looking at you and if the person you guessed does make eye contact.

▶▶ I wonder what song will come on the station next?

▶▶ I wonder if I will see wildlife today? Or that cat?

▶▶ I wonder how many dogs I will see today?

This is a playful game, so have fun with it. Honing your senses of anticipation is useful in and of itself. Anticipation can be read as anxiety in the body, so actively playing this game helps you expand your window of tolerance. Annie Wright, LMFT, a licensed psychotherapist and relational trauma recovery specialist, has this to say about the window of tolerance:

> *"The 'Window of Tolerance' is a term coined by Daniel J. Siegel, a clinical professor of psychiatry at the UCLA School of Medicine, to describe the optimal emotional "zone" we can exist in, to best function and thrive in everyday life. The Window of Tolerance—the optimal zone—is characterized by a sense of groundedness, flexibility, openness, curiosity, presence, an ability to be emotionally regulated, and a capacity to tolerate life's stressors."*[9]

Imagine the window of tolerance as the space you get to grow and improve as you are able to tolerate more expansive situations with people, places, and things. For example, when you are burned out, overwhelmed, and have reached max capacity, your window of tolerance will be small. You may be able to get the dishes done and make your bed while going grocery shopping or interfacing with people is not an option. Then, with rest, delegation, sleep, movement, and nutrition tweaks, your window of tolerance becomes more expansive. You can clean the whole house, go to a friend's party, and have energy for planning. The window of tolerance ebbs and flows in response to how well you are managing stress and healing trauma.

Wright continues by saying, "*Rather, the goal is to expand our Window of Tolerance and to grow our capacity to 'rebound and be resilient'—coming back to our window quickly and effectively when we find ourselves outside it.*" Re-condition yourself to become comfortable with anticipatory energy. Being comfortable with anticipatory energy is an important skill in life, especially if you have to defend yourself or problem-solve in an emergency. Having an established channel in your internal defence structure that can

---

[9] Annie. (2025, January 29). *What is The Window of Tolerance and why is it so important?* Annie Wright - *Your Guide to Relational Trauma Recovery.* https://anniewright.com/window-of-tolerance/

anticipate both good and bad things is very, very useful. Anticipation is often overlooked, but re-igniting your capacity to handle joy is just as important as being prepared to handle stress.

Tip #3 Delay reaching for your cell phone

Start with five minutes and increase little by little until you can get to one hour. Having liminal space, the in-between space without input or thoughts, is wonderful. You will be able to hear your own thoughts and learn how to feel safe without stimuli. This conditions your mind to self-soothe. I know this can be incredibly hard, especially if you have C-PTSD or anxiety. Scrolling and having others' thoughts and images in your mind space can feel like a relief. This tip is to practice hearing what YOUR thoughts are and feeling into YOUR self, without added noise. The liminal space of self, just being, helps you establish trust that you can check in with your self at the start of your day or the end of the night. Five minutes to start, set a timer and increase as your window of tolerance expands. Once you do it once, you can do it again. Baby steps.

Tip #4 Meditate

▶▶ Listening to guided meditations will help you anchor your awareness into your body, provided you are using a body guided meditation.

This can help you with your wonderment of how you feel, by asking you to feel into your toes, your shoulders, etc. It will condition your mind to allow self-discovery and guide you into feeling into the body. A body relaxation meditation is a good place to start.

Tip #5 Inner Child Healing

▶▶ Guided meditations for healing the inner-child

▶▶ Dedicated Journal prompts for Inner child healing

➤ What would happen if you said no growing up?

➤ What would happen if you brought up something that you didn't feel right about?

➤ How did your parents treat you when you were direct?

➤ What does it feel like in your body when you ask a direct question?

Dedicated Journal Affirmations for Inner Child Healing

▶▶ I now have the right process, and I have the right to take steps and make mistakes.

▶▶ I do not have to have immediate perfection. This might not have been true when I was little, but it is true now.

▶▶ I have the right to how I see things, even if others don't see them the way I do! This might not have been true when I was little, but it is true now.

▶▶ Nature gave me a natural intuition, and I am now honouring it. That wasn't possible growing up. I am changing that now.

▶▶ I can tolerate being misunderstood. That wasn't true when I was growing up.

▶▶ I can tolerate disagreements now. This might not have been allowed before, but it is true now.

Tip #6 Do a body practice

To listen to the body, you must live in your body. Move your body to new inputs; soften, expand, release, and challenge the body to withstand force outside of itself. Withstanding force is the opposite of a passive mode of being. If you have played badminton, you have to receive force of impact in your knees, hips, and pelvis. You rotate the torso and receive impact in the arms while swinging the racket. Moving the body unlocks the treasures and trauma stored in the tissues. Both reveal a greater capacity to feel. Moving your body does not need to be complicated. I am a huge advocate for a dedicated practice, as I have over three decades logged, receiving force from yoga therapy and jiu-jitsu inputs. I know how pivotal body practice is for you to learn how to listen to your body.

You can try:

> Yoga or Yoga therapy
> Tai chi
> Jiu Jitsu
> Somatic Experiencing
> Golf
> Work out and sweat!
> Dance

> Tennis
> Pickleball
> Badminton
> Curling
> Bowling
> Swing on a swing

Sara, my 80-year-old student, shows up every week to move her body and receive inputs in yoga therapy. Sara, moving consistently with a felt sense, has expanded her window of tolerance for tricky interpersonal relationships. For years, her relationship with her brother was strained. What she initially intuited as a gut punch when they would relate with each other was revealed to be stored survival responses from a family system that had dysfunctional patterns and low PEMS hygiene. Now, she can manage her boundaries with her brother and listen to her gut instincts regarding how to have an emotionally safe relationship. Sara is remarkable in how she continues to expand her resilience, heal her mind and body, and create safety within her body, always remarking that she feels ageless on the mat!

We'll cover my preferred body movement practices (yoga and jiu-jitsu) along with other practices you can implement in the Movement is Medicine chapter.

Up next, let's get into your personal protection system; your internal defence system called your nervous system blueprint.

CHAPTER 5

Your Nervous System Blueprint

Nervous system regulation and nervous system healing are about learning a new organizational style for your behaviour. You learn this by discovering how your core needs have been impacted, recognizing what your default survival style is, and creating new pathways for emotional inputs and stimuli in your body! Your core needs for connection, autonomy, trust, attunement, and love have a required baseline that directly influences your survival style.

For example, autonomy is the natural individuation of the self from your mother or caregiver. There are many phases for developmental autonomy, from being a babe to a toddler and the necessary freedom to explore, from a child to a teenager to a young adult. Then there is the autonomy from school, college, work, family life, and independence. Being able to safely individuate from all of these examples is a fundamental practice and one that can cause many opportunities for misalignment and inadequacies.

If you have not had a healthy individuation or autonomy, you may have difficulty with boundaries, and you may not be able to express needs or wants without feeling guilt or shame. Your core developmental needs have a corresponding shame and pride-based identity. For example, a pride-based identity from the core need of autonomy is being sweet, compliant, and leaning into the nice girl programming. I encourage you to look more deeply into this if you have identified developmental trauma. A great resource is the book *Healing Developmental Trauma; How Early Trauma Affects Self-Regulation, Self-Image and the Capacity for Relationships* by Laurence Heller, Ph.D, and Aline LaPierre, Psy.D.

There are positive attributes and negative attributes to having had a healthy or misattuned core need satiated, just as there are positive and negative characteristics with survival responses. We will take a deep dive into survival responses in the upcoming chapter. However, to understand your nervous system blueprint, you need to understand how you developed your survival style, so we'll cover the basics here.

Survival style is based on the four survival responses of fight, flight, freeze, and fawn. You create stored survival responses in the body every time there is a significant alarm or traumatic events that you don't process. The body may become stuck in patterns of fight, flight, freeze, or fawn, creating a stored survival response. Another way to think of this is as somatic stress, trauma, or trapped alarms in the body. These unconscious, distressing alarms become entrenched in your internal defence structure, conditioning your behaviour and your personality and directly influencing your ability to feel safe in your body. When you do not feel safe in your body, you will retreat to your mind.

This pattern of retreat has been happening unconsciously since you were born. But what happens to the sensations or events that caused your retreat? They get stored in your body, ruminating in your nervous system. Your nervous system has been supervising itself, not only since you were in utero, but also carries with it generational timelines and cultural influences. Once you recognize how your body-mind processes and responds to your individual organizational structure, you will know what to do to upgrade your survival style.

Collectively, as a society, we excel at emotional suppression and avoidance. Unwittingly, we have all internalized and celebrated the societal norms of overworking, people-pleasing, and using drugs and alcohol to numb out without realizing that these can be stored survival responses fronting as personality and accepted as societally approved behaviour. Being an adrenaline junkie, micromanaging, workaholism, codependency, over-serving, or over-giving can all be signs of a dysregulated nervous system. That dysregulation originated from unmet core needs and a subsequent faulty warning system that developed as a result. When this happens, maladaptive coping mechanisms replace healthy love and connection and toxic, codependent behaviours replace trust and attunement.

In order to understand your nervous system blueprint (your internal defence system), you need to be initiated into learning a new language. This compels me to teach you the technical aspects of your nervous system. Learning the language of your nervous system is key to being able to regulate it. Reading the technical terms of how the body processes information and stress allows the rational brain to come online because awareness changes consciousness. In other words, when you perceive something, you can influence it. Here's a phrase to frame this in your mind: Name it, to Claim it, so you can Influence it. Name it to tame it, also works.

When you perceive something, you can influence it.

Your nervous system works by detecting information received from your senses, organizing that intelligence, and activating a seemingly appropriate response to the data. Another way to think about your nervous system is to recognize it as your operating system. This operating system, through the collection of data and preloaded inputs from energy that has never been properly discharged, develops default settings. Those default settings run in the background until you upgrade them. Much like a computer, if you never choose a personal home screen, preferred browser, or set the scroll rate, the factory settings run on default. Your autonomic nervous system (ANS) is your operating system. It comes with pre-installed performance software based on your interactions with people, places, and things. There are preloaded software systems that were loaded before you could speak or understand language. Your body, your nervous system, records everything you see, hear, and experience, including during your preverbal phase of life, from when you were a wee babe right up to this moment, right now. There are inputs and programs that get installed in school, from friends, from family, from work, all running in the background, unconsciously, in your psyche.

Until you can recognize those pre-loaded, default programs running in the background, you will respond to people, places, and things based on those inputs. Your nervous system will be set to autopilot. Are you beginning to see that without looking under the metaphoric hood of your operating system, you may be behaving in ways that are heavily influenced by unmet core needs? You cannot consistently gauge your behavioural responses until you understand your survival responses.

To regulate your nervous system, you need to fix the faulty warning system that has been popping off under the surface of your consciousness.

Now that you recognize you have an old operating system running, you can learn how to reboot and upgrade your nervous system. To regulate your nervous system, you need to fix the faulty warning system that has been popping off under the surface of your consciousness. To repair this wiring, you are going to restore proper functioning between the rational and emotional brains so you can feel in charge of how you respond to life. You are going to learn how to feel safe feeling your body again.

When you are threatened, stressed, or out of alignment, emotionally or physically, your first innate protection strategy is called the social engagement system (SES). We learned this social engagement system intuitively and unconsciously from when we were babies. When something was wrong, we would cry, and we were then soothed by a caregiver. This SES is the initial mechanism for our core needs being satisfied, engaging others around us to receive connection, trust, love, attunement, and autonomy. As a defenceless babe, you had to rely on your environment and the people within it to soothe, calm and reassure you. Your SES is registering input on an unconscious basis through your psyche, picking up cues, facial gestures, energy, and support.

As adults, we rely on this same mechanism. When we are distressed, we seek out others to help us calm down through communication, gestures, reassurances, and/or just being able to vent and be heard. The SES works automatically based on your history of caregivers responding in a supportive way. Conversely, if those caregivers are the source of distress and your core needs were not satisfied, your social engagement system becomes wounded.

Your next line of protection deployed when you are stressed, in danger, or out of alignment is the limbic system—your emotional governess or emotional nervous system. Here, in the limbic system, your memories, emotions, behaviours, motivations, and autonomic nervous system are managed. The limbic system supervises your actions based on what it learns from your environment, specifically the hypothalamus, which is a tiny region at the base of the brain. The hypothalamus will set off an alert system in the body for a fight, flight, or freeze response. This is a healthy, normal response of your nervous system. Having a fight-or-flight response is how we have survived for centuries. This internal protection system was designed to alert us in the face of danger (we'll cover it in more detail in the chapter on survival responses). It also just so happens to respond the same to a real threat as it does to a perceived threat.

A perceived threat, for example, is hearing the bark of a large dog while you are out on a morning walk. The hypothalamus switches on from the amygdala (another part of the limbic system), sending out a distress signal and causing the adrenal glands to light up, releasing a surge of hormones like epinephrine, adrenaline, and cortisol into the bloodstream. The pupils dilate, your sense of sight and sound becomes heightened, the heart beats faster, pushing blood to the extremities, and the cortisol that was released means your body can be stronger for fighting or faster for fleeing. Small airways in the lungs open wide, bringing in as much oxygen as possible with each breath. All of these changes happen so quickly that most people aren't aware of them. In fact, this protective wiring is so efficient that the limbic system (specifically the amygdala and hypothalamus) initiates this rapid, cascading response before the brain's visual centres have had a chance to fully process what is happening. This automatic response to kick in gear lends itself to the name: autonomic nervous system response.

The autonomic nervous system is the network of nerves throughout your entire body that receives information from either external stimuli or from inside the body. It responds to perceived threats the same way it does to real danger. It does not discriminate. The ANS controls the unconscious processes of your body. And not just any processes, but ones that keep you alive, like your heart beating, breathing, your ability to rest and digest, and your fight-or-flight instinct. The problem with chronic dysregulation is that you can just as easily initiate a fight-or-flight response from having too many emails in your inbox as you would to a bear being on your porch.

You see, our brains have a negativity bias. This bias means we are more likely to pay attention to threats than we are to safety. This bias is compounded by the autonomic nervous system, your main operating system that has been pre-loaded with software from the culmination of your life experiences and has organized itself as a result. Going back to the computer metaphor, all the stored survival responses and trapped alarms act as pre-loaded templates or default storage. Remember, these are from not being able to discharge or actualize the instinct for fight, flight, freeze, or fawn.

Stored survival responses, trapped alarms, and somatic stress are all interchangeable. I use these descriptions intentionally so you can bring your awareness to how your body has registered your unique interpersonal experiences. Whether you have had an impact on your core needs or suffered from accidents, chronic illness, surgery, injury, or even been under anaesthesia, it's almost certain you have developed somatic stress. This is why you need to regulate your nervous system.

Your body has 100 billion neurons, or nerve cells, that connect throughout the entire body. The autonomic nervous system has three branches or parts:

1. **Sympathetic Nervous System**: The system responsible for your body's fight-or-flight response. This system activates body processes that help you in times of need, especially times of stress and danger.

2. **Parasympathetic Nervous System:** The system responsible for the rest-and-digest response. This system is the opposite of your sympathetic nervous system and cannot be on at the same time. This means that if you are stressed (activated by a flight-or-fight response) you are not chilling and resting and digesting. Vice versa, when your parasympathetic nervous system is activated, you are calm and not in a heightened fight-or-flight response.

3. **Enteric Nervous System:** This is a special division of the autonomic nervous system, found in the gut. It is the most complex neural network outside of your brain. With more than 500 million neurons in this system alone, it is unique. It can operate somewhat independently from your brain and central

nervous system. This system can gather information from your GI tract, process that information, and generate a response without sending the information back to your brain! The enteric nervous system is referred to as the *second brain* or *gut-brain*!

It's also important to mention the vagus nerve, which is the main link between your gut-brain (enteric nervous system) and your brain-brain. An outstanding 80%[10] of the fibres of this nerve send messages directly from the body to the brain, not the other way around. Your gut microbes are constantly sending chemical signals to your brain. This means your body interprets data, reactions, emotions, and interpersonal situations and responds accordingly. The information that you respond to is influenced by the body. This is bottom-up information—from the body to the brain—NOT top-down information—from the brain to the body! This is why having a practice that helps you resolve the issues in your tissues is paramount to healing your PEMS systems and nervous system regulation.

Your brain and your gut talk to each other!

Your brain and your gut talk to each other! Gut feelings, butterflies in your stomach, gut-wrenching, trust your gut…these are all examples of the bestie relationship your brain and your gut have! This massive neural network is not just responsible for digestion, but your decision making, stress levels, emotions, and gut instincts.

Why did I name this book *Gut Punch*? Because more information passes between your brain and your gut than any other body system.

Now, I need to make the distinction that the nervous system only heals through feelings, not thoughts. Makes sense, *doesn't it*? You can actually feel the stored survival responses in your body. Where do you wear

---

[10] Mandalaneni, K., Rayi, A. *Vagus nerve stimulator*. StatPearls [Internet]. 2020 Aug 20. https://www.ncbi.nlm.nih.gov/books/NBK562175/

your stress? Shoulders? Neck? Tummy? You know what it feels like to have worn stress patterns in your body. What you are feeling are the cumulative, stored survival responses. The mind is far too clever and self-protective; it will tell you anything you want. The body knows; the body feels everything. This is why we have to feel the feelings and not just think the thoughts.

I am going to describe what it used to feel like for me when I tried to avoid feeling my feelings. Don't get me wrong, dysregulation still happens, and I still get triggered, but my capacity to tolerate stress and my awareness to process (actually feeling) has gotten hella better. Regulation does not imply that you will never try to outsmart your feelings or that you will become a zen monk who lives in a net zero vibe, never bothered or agitated. Getting agitated, angry, sad, frustrated, disappointed, etc., are all normal responses to people, places, and things. Giving you glimpses into some of the ways my dysregulation occurs may spark an understanding of your processing.

This is from a blog post I wrote about one of my trigger episodes:

When I have been triggered or been in an uncomfortable situation, I try to control my mind and think out my emotions. Cognitively, I will rationalize what is happening and look for solutions and remedies. I will keep hashing out thoughts, scenarios, and opinions while my body initiates her fight-or-flight-or-freeze response, protecting herself, subconsciously, from the perceived threat that triggered me. I will convince myself that I am fine, it is all fine, all the while suppressing my emotions and ignoring the sensations in my body.

And before I know it, it is 2 am, and even though I meditated, took some extra magnesium, and watched a show to calm and distract myself, the adrenaline is still pumping, and the limbic train has definitely left the station. This is what dysregulation feels like for me, at any rate. My breathing becomes shallow, my body feels tight, and I either need to stretch and move or be as still as possible. What first presents as various muscle aches radiates into my armpit and down my left leg, specifically lodging itself behind my knee. It is then that I recognize my dysregulation is developing into anxiety. My body has received an impact. She registered the threat as immediate and responded in kind.

My mind was so clever, thinking she could get herself out of it, that she ignored the body. And the body always wins. She keeps score[11] of all of it! Dysregulation can happen sneakily. Dysregulation doesn't mean you did something wrong! Not at all! It will happen over and over again, granting you the ability to be swifter, more inclusive in your multi-awareness strategies, and kinder to yourself, knowing the opportunity for change and growth is ever present. The more readily you learn to intentionally dislodge the outdated defence structure and heal the somatic stress in your body-mind, the quicker you can heal. You don't need to be stuck in a never-ending feedback loop of faulty alarm systems and chronic dysregulation like I was for decades.

You do not have to tackle all your unmet core needs and get tangled in your wounding.

The body is what you must reawaken. Feel to heal. I know it can feel scary, dear heart. You may have learned that the body is not safe. You may think the mind is your escape. This is not how you will heal; you have to resolve the issues in your tissues. Unlike the Hollywood version of a cascading floodgate opening

---

[11] The massively popular book, *The Body Keeps the Score: Brain, Mind and Body in the Healing of Trauma* by Bessel van der Kolk, M. D., and published by Penguin Books is a wonderful read. Dr. van der Kolk has spent over 3 decades using scientific methods to show how trauma literally reshapes both body and brain. He advocates using an integrated healing approach of movement and mindfulness to develop neurofeedback loops that improve our relationships that hurt and heal.

that envelops your whole being, nervous system regulation is more like a slow drip. It is drops of water that slowly penetrate the hardened, shut-down states of being. For example, it is quite common to stop listening to your body and following its instinctive clues at your most primal basics.

To do this work, you **do not have to** tackle all your unmet core needs and get tangled in your wounding. You start with awarenessing, which we'll cover in detail later. Re-ignite your instinct to follow your biological impulses. How? Simple: Notice the urge to empty your bladder and then go to the bathroom. Notice when you need to sleep, and make time to sleep or have a nap. Notice when you are thirsty and have a drink of water. These basic needs, when answered, can help you attune to the body's requirements instead of the habitual default of overriding what you need at the moment.

You have been conditioned to deny your basic needs in lieu of finishing a task, getting to another location, or making more time. Worst of all, you've lost the habit of giving yourself permission to listen to what your body needs. Remember being in school and having to ask to go to the bathroom? Ingrained responses of denial run deep.

Nervous System Regulation

Nervous system regulation is a brilliant practice and one that you can practice all on your own. You get to be the subject, practitioner, and teacher. You can learn this new language system and practice the techniques all by yourself. Having a supportive therapist, pet, family, and/or friend around you to co-regulate is important, but it is not always readily available. It is vital that you know you can practice this with autonomy and independence from others. The bottom line here is that if you understand all the contributing factors to what is in your operating system, you can give yourself radical self-compassion and try something new.

From what you have read, I am sure you can see all the many ways you would've developed layers upon layers of avoidance in your nervous system. Naturally, the depth of this stratum lies deep beneath the veil of consciousness, buried in your psyche. To unearth these blankets of intertwined emotional, mental, physical, and spiritual wires requires your intent and your attention. Bring your awareness to why you think the way you do. What do you have resistance to, and how can you increase your capacity to tolerate higher thresholds of experience? This is how you regulate your nervous system. Invite yourself to have a continual, base inquiry: *What am I feeling right now? Why am I feeling the things I am feeling?* Once you begin the self-enquiry as to why you think and feel what you do, you can pinpoint when your baseline gets charged or activated. Feeling your feelings is not always easy. Feelings can be hella scary, especially if you have been in a chronic shutdown or suspended freeze mode.

Your body built your internal defence system to protect you before you had awareness. Having a regulated nervous system does not mean you do not experience polarity or being off-balance. It means you can navigate stress more easily. It means you can experience a sense of safety, ease, curiosity, productivity, and creativity. A regulated nervous system is reflected in your capacity to live in the present. It represents your resiliency—the resiliency for managing the ups and downs of this complicated business of being alive. A regulated nervous system expands your capacity for emotional depth and connection to self. It brings with it a healthier body, one that has been able to discharge the adrenalized stress responses. You feel a coherence in your PEMS hygiene system. Take heart, dear one; you are allowed to be safe, you are allowed to express your feelings, and you are allowed to reorganize your internal protection system.

Within this book are techniques to teach you how to release self-limiting beliefs to re-organize your mind-body. You can learn how to self-soothe the alarm system, discharge negative experiences, and retrain your brain. Your brain is a learning machine and, as we covered earlier, it is not a fixed state, as once believed.

Due to neuroplasticity, your lovely brain and, by extension, your nervous system have this amazing ability to adapt, giving you freedom of choice when you experience interpersonal difficulties. This ability of the brain to form new connections and pathways and change how its circuits are wired means that your brain is adaptable and malleable to inputs, rewards, experiences, successes, and pitfalls. Brains can change after a person has reached adulthood! How awesome is that? Especially for those of us who have anxiety, trauma, high ACE scores, and C-PTSD. Your brain is able to recalibrate itself in the presence of new thoughts, behaviours, and responses to your environment. In the same way you can learn to re-organize your response to emotional inputs in your nervous system, the brain itself can be re-routed and re-established to support new habits. Neuroplasticity helps you to create a version of yourself that supports safety! The process of neuroplasticity means you are not stuck with the default settings of your internal defence system; you can change how your nervous system responds to people, places, and things.

Brains can change after a person has reached adulthood!

As Christopher Bergland, author of *The Athlete's Way*, writes:

> *"One could speculate that this process opens up the possibility to reinvent yourself and move away from the status quo or to overcome past traumatic events that evoke anxiety and stress. Hardwired fear-based memories often lead to avoidance behaviours that can hold you back from living your life to the fullest."*[12]

---

[12] Christopher Bergland, (2017) *The Athlete's Way: Sweat and the Biology of Bliss.* St. Martin's Press.

Knowing that your brain can change will help you on your journey to reclaiming agency over your body, your mind, your emotions, and your being!

CHAPTER **6**

Trauma Is a Stored Survival Response

*"Healing trauma is less about talking it
and more about feeling through it"*
–Dr. Russell Kennedy

When someone experiences trauma, it activates the stress response in the body, elevating hormones and disrupting the normal functioning of the brain. When someone has unresolved trauma in their body-mind, it creates a barrier to feeling or hearing their gut instincts or intuition. The stored trauma will mute or blur the intuitive knowing without conscious thought because of the activated stress response that fires off when triggered. Stored trauma can occur in a myriad of ways, one of which is not being soothed or cared for in the face of a traumatic experience. The most common psychological stress responses to trauma are fight, flight, freeze, and fawn. If you cannot fulfill the outcome or psychological response to a person, place, or thing, this will cause the traumatic experience to become stored in the mind-body—into your cells and tissue. The issues in your tissues are the stored survival responses that were never actualized. If you wanted to fight but couldn't or if you wanted to leave but didn't—these are examples of how the stress response gets stored.

Trauma can cause persistent stress and chronic states of anxiety in the mind-body. It is not necessarily the event that happened but rather what gets imprinted or stored in the body as a result of the traumatic event.

Trauma can show up or look like:

- ✦ Anxiety and or chronic overwhelm
- ✦ Hypervigilance
- ✦ Being easily triggered
- ✦ Insomnia
- ✦ Flashbacks or intrusive thoughts
- ✦ Difficulty connecting
- ✦ Anger
- ✦ Self Sabotage
- ✦ Depression
- ✦ Negative thought patterns
- ✦ People pleasing/fawning

Dr. Russel Kennedy[13] has coined an appropriate acronym to describe trapped survival responses for situations and occurrences that can cause trauma in the body. He calls them alarms, which is brilliant because the alarm goes off due to a traumatic event, but what happens after the alarm is sounded? More often than not, nothing to resolve the alarm. Thus, it gets stored or trapped in the body.

---

[13] Dr. Russell Kennedy's book, Anxiety Rx published by Awaken Village Press, October 2020

Dr. Kennedy's ALARMS stands for:

A Any physical, emotional, or sexual abuse

L Loss, including toys, pets, loved ones

A Abandonment, either emotional or physical

R Rejection by loved ones or friends, being bullied or ridiculed

M Maturing too early, being parentified, using drugs and alcohol, having sex too early, carrying the burden of responsibility too early

S Shame, things that a child or adult perceives as shameful

Parentified is when a child is forced to take on the responsibilities of an adult, either emotionally or physically. If a parent or caregiver was absent in their role to provide security and safety for you as a child, this can cause developmental issues. Some qualities may be beneficial, like becoming a good caregiver or having responsibility. Not so good qualities are feeling like you never had a childhood, not being able to play or let loose, and feeling like your worth is directly tied to your output.

Trauma can be described as an emotional or psychological response to a distressing event or experience that is overwhelming. Big T trauma typically refers to a cataclysmic event or events that, by majority consensus, are considered serious. Big T trauma can include sexual violence, abuse, assault, rape, warfare, sudden loss of a loved one, or a major accident or injury. Little t trauma typically refers to distressing events that have a varied causality between experiencers, meaning it is case- and person-specific and not as serious as life-threatening experiences. Emotional mis-attunement, minor injury, break-ups, and discordant relationships can all cause little t trauma. Both can cause long-lasting effects on an individual's emotional, physical, spiritual, and mental well-being and can lead to conditions like PTSD (post-traumatic stress disorder).

PTSD became known in the collective lexicon as something soldiers endured during war. Originally coined "nostalgia" by an Austrian physician named Josef Leopold, in 1761, he observed soldiers who had been exposed to military trauma as having sleep problems, anxiety, missing home, and feeling deeply sad. By 1919, "shell shock" was coined to describe this military trauma. In 1952, "gross stress reaction," a precursor to PTSD, was added to the Diagnosis and Statistical Manual of Mental Disorders, or DSM. This is an apt description, but it didn't take into consideration the long-lasting effects. The disorder did not resolve itself in six months, as was initially believed. In fact, many people never recovered from having symptoms. Finally, in 1980, PTSD was added to the DSM.

I illustrate the evolution of diagnosing trauma to show how difficult understanding the symptoms of trauma disorders has been for the collective. Understanding how trauma affects our society is an ever-evolving science and one that is fraught with dismissal, glazing over, and invalidation. PTSD describes a condition typically related to a singular, traumatic event, like a burglary or assault. There is also a lesser-known condition called C-PTSD, which is Complex Post Traumatic Stress Disorder. C-PTSD has not yet been added to the DSM. It typically occurs from repeated, sustained, or multiple forms of traumatic events, like repeated abuse from a caregiver, hostage situations, victims of human trafficking, bullying, and/or chronic psychological or physical abuse.

C-PTSD can occur from both big T and little t trauma, though typically, it is seen in people who experienced trauma from a young age or earlier in their development stage. For example, those who were abused by someone they thought they could trust, such as a parental figure or protector. This impacts their nervous system and severely impairs their gut instincts and their ability to form attachments to or relationships with others and even themselves. Big T and little t trauma can overlap, as does the diagnosis for PTSD and C-PTSD. The chart[14] below provides a good visual for the similarities and differences between the two.

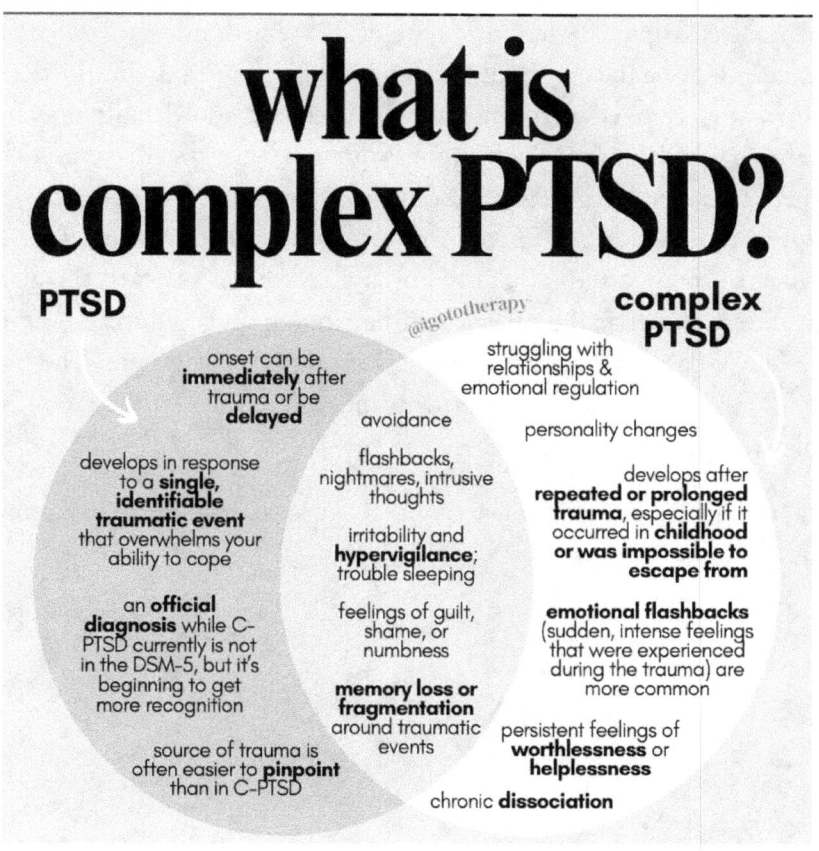

[14] Used with permission. Courtesy of @igototherapy Instagram page. https://www.instagram.com/igototherapy

Trauma has an EFFECT and needs a careful, gentle self-inquiry to re-establish safety in the body.

The important takeaway is that trauma has an EFFECT and needs a careful, gentle self-inquiry to re-establish safety in the body. You absolutely can recreate safety within your mind-body, but before you can build up your resilience, you need to understand the impact that stored trauma creates.

Stored trauma disables the healthy functioning of your internal defence system. It corrupts the nervous system and whittles down your ability to determine what you should welcome and what you should defend against. The trapped survival responses become the default operating system in your hardware, meaning your nervous system responds to triggers before you can even become consciously aware of them. This is why implementing a PEMS routine is vital to nurturing your gut instincts. When you know that you may have never resolved the alarm, you understand that that alarm will be ringing and polluting everyday experiences based on outdated wiring in your nervous system. The issues in your tissues have been damaged, truncated, and re-routed away from resolution, peace, and resilience.

As a reminder, you can have trapped survival responses (unresolved trauma) from:

✧ Injury

✧ Medical interventions

✧ Death of a loved one

✧ Loss of a pet

✧ Rejection

✧ Abandonment

✧ Chronic illness

✧ Motor vehicle accidents

✧ Surgery

Trapped or stored survival responses cause chronic stress and anxiety in the mind-body. Amber, my yoga therapy client, was convinced she didn't have any trauma growing up. Yet, Amber has irritable bowel syndrome, insomnia, chronic neck pain flare-ups, and drinks heavily on occasion. She never understood that the demands of her family system, the rivalry with her siblings, and her youth spent in competitive gymnastics all contributed to a dysregulated PEMS system. The family system she was born into impacted her internal defence structure, which created a psycho-somatic connection. Her gut was off because she had unresolved trauma from her youth. Initially, there was no Big T or little t trauma that she could pinpoint, but it was there nonetheless.

Amber spent her youth denying her body's natural rhythm and continued this theme as an adult, pursuing a career in front of a camera. She could not respond to the three most prevalent stress responses of flight, fight, or freeze and compensated by employing an elaborate fawn/people-pleasing response. Until she allows her body to express itself, overwriting years of denial for the pursuit of output, she will have unresolved trauma trapped in her tissues. Luckily, Amber is also a very astute, inquisitive learner and has begun to elevate her consciousness around the PEMS hygiene system to re-create safety within.

Like Amber, I, too, had to heal my fragmented sense of self so I could learn how to rely on my internal compass and re-learn how to trust my gut. Unresolved trauma and C-PTSD can cause feelings of guilt, shame, and worthlessness that cloud intuition and distort your authentic self-expression for decades or until you heal the issues in your tissues. Learning how to love yourself unconditionally and radical self-acceptance are key to resolving trauma. This takes time, but it *works*, and it *will work* for you, dear heart!

I know from experience that healing trauma is a complex and uniquely individual journey. What worked for me might not entirely work for you. You have to try many modalities and practices to see what resonates with you. It is my hope that this book gives you a variety of solutions that you can play with.

The starting point is to have the desire for healing. To have a desire to live with reduced reactivity. Then, once the desire is in place, we implement a PEMS routine, put in the work, anticipate setbacks, and keep going. No one thing or bio hack will suffice. There are no silver bullets to healing trauma or regulating the nervous system. You cannot cold plunge or just breathe your way back from trauma. It takes conscious awareness, a multi-layered approach, incorporating bodywork, therapy, community, radical self-acceptance, and time to release the stored survival responses trapped inside your mind-body. Rebuilding trust within yourself rewires your internal self-defence system, and once you get it back, you will be incentivized to keep it! You can relearn how to trust your gut, *even after trauma.*

Following your intuition and hearing your gut instincts requires you to be attuned to your internal wisdom. When you are in constant survival mode and have a chronic stress response, your ability to access the wisdom of your gut is greatly hindered. Traumatic experiences can lead to dissociation, a freeze response which is a defence mechanism that makes individuals detach or separate from their sensations, emotions, or even their sense of self. The individual can become shut down, immobilized, and numb. Dissociation can fragment the flow of thoughts and feelings, creating a disconnection from intuitive hints or cues. It is a protective mechanism (that can be a blessing) when trauma occurs. The problem is when dissociation becomes ingrained in the nervous system as a coping mechanism, pulling a person further away from resolution and developing resiliency. I have dissociative episodes on the mat whilst doing jiu-jitsu still to this day. It is a well-honed defence mechanism that I deploy when over-stimulated, triggered, or severely uncomfortable. I share this with you because healing trauma is not a straight line or a linear task that you can complete with a virtual check mark and never have a recurrence.

My dissociative episodes are positive at times and negative at other times. Knowing I have them is the awareness that can create change. When Amber realized she had trauma from her faulty family system, she could implement changes that supported finding a resolution for herself. She no longer berated herself for the past heavy drinking; understanding it was a defence mechanism that was, thankfully, unsustainable and unsatisfying.

Accepting that unresolved trauma is pervasive in society and having these faulty alarm systems sounding off in the mind-body interrupts the ability to create safety in the body. Without safety, it is really hard to listen to your gut and interface with the world around you, and you need to create this safety in each of the PEMS areas. In the words of Will Van Derveer, MD,[15] co-founder of the Integrative Psychiatry Institute, "As a psychiatrist, I learned early in my career that a psychological approach to mental health is incomplete. Similarly, a purely physical approach is incomplete. Further, a spiritual approach is incomplete. We need to address all areas of well-being."

---

[15] Quoted from Dr. Sara Gottfried's book, *The Autoimmune Cure*, Published by Harpers Collins, 2024.

CHAPTER 7

Survival Responses

This chapter focuses on the four F's[16] of psychological survival responses and the subsequent emotional, behavioural, and defensive styles that develop. These are not to be confused with attachment styles, which I would encourage you to look up and investigate further. Given my high ACE score and C-PTSD diagnosis, learning how the autonomic nervous system was organizing inputs based on my misattunement catapulted my healing. The important thing to remember as you go through this chapter is that these are just patterns, and you can change them. You are not stuck with these patterns. They are not *you*! Remember: Your mind can change your body. Your body can change your mind. Your behaviour changes the outcome.

Your nervous system accesses three places for regulation:

1. Social Engagement System

2. Mobilize Fight or Flight response (sympathetic branch of your autonomic nervous system)

3. Freeze response (parasympathetic branch of your ANS).

[16] The breakdown of these 4F survival responses are from Pete Walker's Book, *Complex PTSD: From Surviving To Thriving* -Azure Coyote Publishing (December 18, 2013)

It's important to note that the Fawn response is not a nervous system response. It is a behavioural response, but just as valid in regulation attempts.

Now that you know where these responses come from, here's a quick reminder of each:

Fight	When you aggressively or physically respond to a threat.
Flight	When you flee from a threat.
Freeze	When you shut down and become immobilized by a threat.
Fawn	When you default to people-pleasing to avoid conflict.

I describe the cycle of emotional dysregulation as an unconscious system of disorganization based on pre-installed inputs. This system needs to be interrupted. The cycle needs to be re-routed into the conscious psyche so you can respond to inputs in a way that doesn't put you in an unsafe feedback loop. Resolving a faulty feedback loop helps you distinguish what is intuition and what is trauma showing up. It allows you to hear your internal voice and not the emotional flashbacks fronting as your gut instincts. This takes time and repetition. Knowing how it works gives you the tools you need to dismantle the loop, reroute, and relearn so you can react in real time.

A cycle of emotional dysregulation looks like this:

1. Interpersonal conflict arises, and you get triggered. This reminds you of a core need not being actualized or a stored alarm like rejection, abandonment, or misattunement. This leads to a conditioned emotional response.

2. Emotional dysregulation is activated (anger, fear, shame).

3. Problematic behaviour arises (dissociation, self-injury, rage).

4. Temporary relief arrives (maladaptive coping mechanisms kick in, people back off, and you get a reprieve from the emotional pain).

5. Interpersonal conflict arises, and then the cycle begins again.

Keep in mind, in step 4, the temporary relief reduces the adrenalized energy but does not soothe the nervous system in a sustainable way. This means that, yes, a glass of wine and a smoke will calm you down, but there is no conscious pattern recognition to interrupt and displace. A maladaptive coping mechanism is a short-term solution that, in my experience, prolongs the process of healing the nervous system because you suspend your feelings. You impose an altered state that tricks you into thinking you are okay, but really, the use of drugs and alcohol has simply made you feel good.

Of course, moderation is key, and I understand how substantial a social cocktail can be to help shift from work life to play life. The emphasis I wish to make is if you consistently rely on drugs and alcohol to alter your state of mind—if it becomes a crutch or the only way that you can downshift—I would encourage you to wonder if it is really helping. Is it the long-term solution? Is it being used to avoid feeling your feelings?

I was a chronic cannabis user for decades, and though it gave me mind space and pain relief and worked for a long time, when it stopped working, I stopped using it. I became anxious when I smoked, which is the opposite of the desired effect, and I realized all the feelings I thought I was resolving were still there. My trapped alarms were subdued and placated while I used cannabis, but the gaps between all my unmet core needs were still there. The same with alcohol. It suddenly made me anxious and gave me a headache. I have been sober since 2018 and credit my sobriety for being able to access deeper levels of nervous system regulation.

Here's an example of what a cycle of emotional dysregulation could look like:

You are having lunch, and you see a mother reprimand her daughter. She grabs her daughter's hand forcefully, pulling her away from the counter. The conflict lasts three minutes; the daughter is upset, and the mother is overwhelmed. You go back to your desk, and you get an alert that a staff meeting will happen in five minutes. During the staff meeting, your ideas are shot down, and you are challenged to qualify your viewpoint. You go home, and your boyfriend wants to surprise you with a night out. You bark at him for being insensitive, and you quarrel. He goes out, and you self-isolate by watching a TV show, shutting off your phone so you don't see his messages, and eating a frozen dinner, followed by a bottle of wine. He comes home to you pretending to be asleep. In the morning, you make him coffee and breakfast and are upbeat and cheery. You do not mention last night, you may or may not apologize, and you go on with a new day.

This cycle of emotional dysregulation, as well as others, can be seen in the following depictions of survival styles and accompanying behaviours. Similar to attachment styles, you develop your survival style based on your brain's (nervous system's) mechanism for tracking and monitoring safety and is influenced by the availability of people, places, and things. Your survival style is correlated to how well and often your core needs were and are satisfied. This information is presented so you can gain a deeper awareness of who you are and why you behave the way you do. Do not feed your inner critic when you read through these or reinforce critical self-judgment as you learn your survival style. When you name it, you can claim it, and then you can influence it. Name it to tame it! Your window of tolerance will expand as will your range of resiliency. When you see what default states operate within yourself, you can choose new behaviours of responses, customizing your internal operating system.

When you name it, you can claim it.

You're about to receive a lot of information, and it might be overwhelming at first. You don't need to try to take in and remember every single thing. However, you should aim, at the very least, to gain some insight into how your automatic internal defence system is currently organized. For you to accurately read what your intuition says, versus how your trauma shows up, it is useful to decode what your survival style may be. Keep in mind that you most likely have a mixed style, like a blend of fight and fawn or a combination of freeze and flight. Read through the information here and see what hits. Look for what lands or reads as your default. You can use this as a guide for future behaviour and emotional expressions as well. Meaning for example, if you find yourself procrastinating and being irritable, you could take a moment to check in: Are you in a fight survival response pattern? What is going on that you have resistance to?

Each nervous system response, or what has been dubbed the 4F responses, has positive and negative characteristics. Meaning, there are good attributes that can be utilized. These are ancient survival tactics after all, and can still be employed in a regulated state of immediate cause and effect. The flight response is a positive trait when you are in danger, but again, if you cannot actualize the response, you can create a stored survival response. As you read through them, familiarize yourself with common emotional responses, dysregulated behaviours, and what is beneficial if one of these is your default style. Take your time to read through them and I highly recommend that you revisit this section more than once.

Fight Survival Response Patterns

Actions of an Unconscious Fight Response

- ❖ Slamming doors
- ❖ Fist pounding
- ❖ Yelling

❖ Mocking, taunting, shaming others

❖ Attempt to control

❖ Violence

❖ Arguing, vocal growls, or muttering under your breath

❖ Binary Thinking (I must be right, you must be wrong)

FIGHT RESPONSE

Positive Characteristics	Dysregulated Characteristics
• Assertiveness • Boundaries • Courage • Leadership • Self protection and protection of others • Motivation and drive	• Demanding • Condescending • Controlling • Explosive behaviour • Entitlement • Judgement • Bullying • Self harm

Common Fight Emotional Responses or Perpetual, Low-Grade Feelings

❖ Irritability

❖ Aggression

❖ Frustrations

❖ Losing control

❖ Anger

❖ Procrastination

❖ Rage

❖ Demanding

If fight shows up as a stored survival response, you may experience resistance in your body. Resistance to failing, resistance to feeling fear, resistance to allowing someone to get close to you. Shifting the resistance through the body will help. Look at the Gravity Anchor practice in Body Movement Chapter to help invite you back into feeling without resistance.

Discharging resistance in the body is key and actually quite difficult. Resistance creates a feedback loop that you rely on; it will feel safe and familiar. Logically, you may respond that it would be silly to be addicted or drawn to resistance, but the mind-body is a clever system. The mind, specifically, will seek to protect itself. It will choose familiar over new almost every time, even if that is at the expense of your well-being. This is why you must work at this, continually retraining your internal defense system so it serves you. Upgrading your consciousness through this work is called metacognition. Metacognition is having an awareness of what you are thinking.

Negative/Dysregulated Fight Response Can Look Like:

* ❖ Unconsciously driven by the belief that power and control create safety
* ❖ Respond to feelings of abandonment with anger
* ❖ Often needing a scapegoat to unload on
* ❖ Control using intimidation, sarcasm, and/or criticism
* ❖ Using aggression to scare away intimacy

How did it feel to read that section?

The resistance piece, specifically, is so valuable to explore. I realized I had developed a feedback loop of resistance from a crappy childhood. Whether it was a ride somewhere or a preference to be observed, I had to work at convincing my caregivers that I deserved to be considered. I felt resistance in my body and would brace myself for a NO when I asked someone to help me.

If Fight is your default, you will benefit from taking self-initiated time-outs when you feel triggered. Notice when you become overly critical and take a beat, pause, spend time alone, returning your baseline back to safety. Doing grief work is paramount to release this default survival pattern. You are allowed to grieve what was not given to you, what could have been, and what you may have missed out on. You are allowed to grieve a living person or thing just as much as someone or something that has passed on. Instead of obsessing over irksome ticks in a present relationship, redirect your rage or unhappiness towards hurtful childhood experiences that you have not yet released the charge of.

The journal prompts for Inner Child Healing in the Gut Punch chapter are designed to help you with your grief work. If fight shows up as a default pattern for you, releasing fear of abandonment and shame is helpful. Writing rage pages (I teach you this in the next chapter, 'Stop Self Abandoning') is a safe outlet for self-expression that you will benefit from if you identify with the Fight response. Writing out the rage, in safety, knowing it is only for you to release the expressions of anger, sadness, disappointment, or shame, is very therapeutic for this survival response. Be mindful if you have a tendency towards perfectionism and give yourself permission to make a mess. Notice if you project that perfectionism onto others and maybe cut them some slack, observing when and why this pattern shows up. Cultivating empathy goes a long way in helping heal this survival pattern. Working with a coach is helpful for creating new pathways and new thought patterns.

Flight Survival Response Patterns

Actions of an unconscious flight response:

* Obsessive thinking
* Constant Busyness
* Hyperactivity

* Avoidance
* "Let's move on"
* Procrastination
* Perfectionism
* Urgency
* Driven-ness
* Adrenaline Junkie

FLIGHT RESPONSE

Positive Characteristics	Dysregulated Characteristics
• Perseverance • Healthy disengagement; -knows when to walk away • Industriousness • Retreats when conflict puts them in danger • Informed know-how	• Workaholic • Perfectionist • Obsessive/Compulsive • Overthinking • Adrenaline Junkie • Micromanager • Flits from one thing to another

Common FLIGHT Emotional Responses or Perpetual, Low-Grade Feelings:

* Panic
* Overwhelm
* Anxiety
* Worry
* Fear
* Urgency

If flight shows up as a stored survival response, you may experience resistance to self-perceived shame in your body. This can manifest as not feeling good enough, spinning out before you are found out, and vacillating between excessive striving and dropping the ball.

Dysregulated Flight Response Can Look Like:

* Unconsciously driven by the belief perfection creates safety and makes you worthy of love.

* Flees from pain/discomfort with constant busyness.

* When not always doing, flight types worry and plan about doing; they are fretful.

* Use overthinking to distract from the pain of abandonment.

* May pursue reckless behaviours for an adrenaline high.

If Flight is your default, you will benefit from grieving childhood losses and slowing down to feel emotions and sensations. The tools in the Somatic Experiencing chapter help you with slowing down and reintroducing safety in your body. Becoming comfortable with liminal space, the space of non-doing, is key if flight shows up as a survival response. Being able to consciously choose non-doing and releasing the need to be busy constantly helps heal this response. Giving yourself permission to watch a sad movie, read a sad story, and allowing yourself to cry helps heal these trapped survival responses. I want you to feel empowered to practice self-compassion, give yourself a break, and let yourself off the hook, because I know how easy it is to fall into the habit of negative self-talk and recrimination. That inner persecutor voice that runs on autopilot is full of shit and you need constant reminding to not listen to that voice.

To interrupt this default pattern, when anxiety kicks in and you feel the need to do something, try to stand still and do nothing. Give yourself this script: I am (your name), and I feel anxiety right now. I want to move and do (activity), but for this moment, I will name three things I can see. I will name one thing I ate recently. These things are (name them). As you say this script, move your eyes laterally, looking from right to left. The PEMS hygiene toolkit is designed to be a readily available resource for you to tap into and use to regulate your nervous system. I want you to see by the end of this book that these practices can happen alongside your daily living, just like brushing your teeth. Incorporating them into your day-to-day living will help you release the trapped alarms, and override the default behaviours that run on autopilot. You can feel safe again with stillness, dear heart!

Freeze Survival Response Patterns

Actions of an Unconscious Freeze Response:

- Can't make decisions
- Zone out/mindless scrolling
- Can't complete tasks
- Difficulty getting out of bed
- Self-shaming
- Isolation
- Just quit/give up
- Ruminations of self-doubt and mistrust
- Preparing for death

The freeze response is on a spectrum. It does not follow a sequential order or respond in a patterned way of worse to way worse. You can freeze and numb out or shut down and then get scared. This list shows the variables on the spectrum of Freeze.

- Fright
- Helplessness
- Depression
- Numbness
- Dissociation
- Shutting down
- Fainting
- Prepare to die

FREEZE RESPONSE

Positive Characteristics	Dysregulated Characteristics
• Mindfulness • Awareness both conscious and acute • Poised readiness • Calm and Peaceful • Presence • Alone not lonely	• Isolates/Hermit • Withdrawn • Space case • Couch potato • Unmotivated • Afraid of achievement • Hides/Camoflauges

Common Unconscious Freeze Response Emotions:

- Can't make decisions
- Zone out/mindless scrolling
- Can't complete tasks
- Difficulty getting out of bed
- Self-shaming
- Isolation

- ♦ Just quit/give up
- ♦ Ruminations of self-doubt and mistrust
- ♦ Preparing for death

Common FREEZE Emotional Responses or Perpetual, Low-Grade Feelings:

- ♦ Boredom
- ♦ Feeling Blank
- ♦ Helplessness
- ♦ Apathy
- ♦ Numbness
- ♦ Shame
- ♦ "I feel Stuck"/ Stuckness
- ♦ "I can't"
- ♦ Depressive feelings
- ♦ Hopelessness

Being in a state of freeze as a habitual, internal defence can cause you to self-doubt, lack confidence, and be in a state of constriction. You may self-abandon here and deny yourself creative joy or pleasure. Make a point of celebrating yourself every week! Interrupt the pattern of feeling stuck and unworthy by celebrating the little nuances of your life. Creating a list after you have done all the things, just so you can cross everything off the list, can be a mini celebration. Learning how to feel good and accomplished, without the dread of the other shoe dropping, takes practice. Learning how to feel okay when you are expansive is the opposite of constricting energy.

Dysregulated Freeze Response Can Look Like:

♦ Being unconsciously driven by the belief that people are dangerous and solitude is safe.

♦ Triggers cause isolation, hiding, and avoiding human contact/socializing.

♦ Dissociating when overwhelmed; disconnecting from feeling pain.

♦ Seeking refuge through sleeping, scrolling, TV, daydreaming, or video games.

♦ Being less motivated to do trauma recovery work.

♦ Allowing the flaws of others to justify isolation.

If Freeze is your default, you will benefit from having a therapeutic relationship to experience safe, relational healing. This can be with a coach or therapist, or even with a pet. Learning how to co-regulate with others helps you heal this default pattern. I co-regulate on the mat, doing jiu jitsu and yoga therapy. Having a favorite show that you can watch when you have a default freeze state is a reliable, safe way to co-regulate with the fictional characters you may consider friends. Get under a weighted blanket, have soul-nourishing snacks, and watch your show once a day, once a week, or once a month. Truth be told, I have a rotation of shows that are always at the ready for a nervous system tune-up, on the daily. I can sit for 10 minutes and watch my fictional TV buddies, and they soothe my nerves and give me the required energy to go for a walk or bounce up and down.

You may have experienced an extended functional freeze cycle, like I did for decades, so having visual touchstones that you can deploy when the brain is shut down and activities are daunting is amazing. Give yourself permission to audit your childhood and see how adequately your needs were met by your parents. You are allowed to explore how and why these default survival patterns show up for you. Adhering to the basic, primal instincts or messages from your body, such as relieving yourself, quenching your thirst, resting, and eating, helps heal this freeze response. By consciously choosing to listen to the base instincts every day, you are re-creating trust within yourself to show up for yourself, to rely on completing the needs you have, even the most basic ones. Regulation and healing happen with repetitive, conscious choices that help you, rather than harm you. Behaviours that support you, rather than tax you.

Giving yourself permission to re-create safety lends itself to building self-trust, which, if chosen, can lead to trust with others. Feeling over thinking is hard work, I know. That's why I wrote this book in a systemized way, so I could introduce you to these concepts AND provide a multi-systems approach and remedy. The practices in the Somatic Experiencing chapter help you move away from the freeze survival responses. A little goes a long way; a one-degree shift or pivot is how you can achieve success implementing your PEMS hygiene system. Titration (we'll cover titration in the SE chapter), building trust, and expanding your window of tolerance for managing life's inputs is how you successfully regulate a dysregulated nervous system state. You are learning the way out of the looping cycle of overextension, withdrawal, helplessness, and contraction, just by expanding your knowledge bank with these words. Good job!

Fawn Survival Response Patterns

+ People pleasing
+ Codependency
+ No boundaries
+ Constantly apologizing
+ Ignoring your needs
+ Over-Caring/Over-Giving

+ Flatters others

+ Won't say no

+ Denial or Avoidance of Conflict

FAWN RESPONSE

Positive Characteristics	Dysregulated Characteristics
• Love	• People pleaser
• Service	• Doormat
• Compromise	• Boundaryless
• Peace-making	• Over-serving
• Caretaking	• Grovelling
• Fairness	• Loss of self
• Listening	• Over giving
• Meeting the attachment needs of children	• Over listening
	• Say yes-means no

Common FAWN Emotional Responses or Perpetual, Low-Grade Feelings:

+ Unworthy

+ Unloved

+ Resentment

+ Depleted

+ Anxious

+ Disembodied

+ Don't know/hyper focussed on others

Fawning is almost always an unconscious reaction used to avoid feeling triggered or uncomfortable or due to being hyper-aware of not disappointing others. Fawning keeps people constantly seeking the approval of others, feeling anxious and depleted. They become disconnected from their own feelings because they are so focused on others.

Dysregulated Fawn Response Can Look Like:

+ Unconsciously believe that safety, approval, and attachment are gained by being helpful, compliant, and people-pleasing.

+ Parentified behaviour (being programmed to take care of the needs of your parents) that has translated to adulthood with peers and family.

+ Feeling the need to be entertaining, high-achieving, or funny, to have value.

+ Developmentally arrested in the sense of self/little or no access to the authentic self.

+ Giving yourself away by over-listening, over-caring, over-serving, and over-giving. Available to all but self.

If Fawn is your default you will benefit from practicing verbal and emotional self-expression. Use the rage pages to get your feelings on paper, kinetically, intentionally. This fortifies your ability to express how you feel, without confrontation. Practice asserting yourself in safe environments, speaking your preferences and opinions. Recognize when you get uncomfortable and try to sit with the sensation as opposed to over-explain why you chose what you chose or think what you think. You are rebuilding trust in yourself first and foremost, so saying I like sushi when everybody else says pasta and leaving it at that, creates a new baseline of safety and trust. It teaches you that it is safe to state a preference; the emotions and neural pathways create a new pattern and emboldens your confidence.

People around you benefit and rely on your fawning behaviour. It is important to know that breaking this pattern will disappoint people and that accepting that they will be disappointed is okay. Using your PEMS model to self soothe and fortify will help neutralize this default pattern. A tip I can share, is if you self abandon, or use a performative behaviour around someone, you may not actually feel safe with them. If Fawn is a default pattern for you, learning how to be authentic and trust you will not be abandoned is your aim.

There is a whole chapter in this book on learning healthy boundaries that teaches you why the default to fawning happens and how to live more authentically. Take your time building these new inputs!! Call in support from trusted family and friends to plan your strategies for breaking this fawning pattern with others. This could look like having a prep talk about how you want to shift the dynamic and then creating a post talking about how it went, what you felt, and how you can add or subtract the next time. Ask for an accountability partner in a trusted friend who can check in on you when you are visiting home. The check-in is to help you NOT succumb to a fawning response in a family gathering that you may have learned from a young age. Take care of your heart, dear one; trying new things feels icky at the start.

Mixed 4F States

According to Pete Walker, there are few pure types in these 4F survival styles or responses. More likely, you will have a blend of the 4Fs, having a primary, a backup, and then a variation of degrees from mild to extreme. Do not self-judge. Use this information as a tool to reconstruct your internal operating system and rewire your ANS system so your survival style is conscious, deliberate, and actionable, as opposed to unconscious and automatic.

FAWN-FIGHT

▶▶ Struggles with emotional flashbacks.

▶▶ Aggressively tries to help others.

▶▶ Caretaking of others is exemplified and a repetition of being a parentified child.

▶▶ Love Bombs others into conforming.

▶▶ Seeks real intimacy more than other types.

FIGHT-FAWN

▶▶ Combines narcissism and codependency. Fluctuates between attacking and over-caring or concern.

▶▶ Caretaking feels coercive and manipulative.

▶▶ In extreme cases, it can be borderline personality disorder.

▶▶ Rarely takes responsibility for interpersonal dynamics.

▶▶ Tendency to project imperfection on others.

▶▶ Devoid of real empathy or compassion.

FLIGHT-FREEZE

▶▶ Finds safety in "do it yourself," isolation, and toxic independence.

▶▶ Works to complete exhaustion, then collapses and vegges out.

▶▶ May be misdiagnosed with Aspergers.

▶▶ May be computer addicts who work for long hauls then dissociate substances/games or excessive sleeping.

FIGHT-FREEZE

▸▸ Cycles through severe isolation and bullying others to meet needs.

▸▸ Extreme social withdrawal.

▸▸ Demands things to go their way but is disinterested in human connection.

▸▸ Can dominate relationships with foul moods and doesn't allow others to speak.

FAWN-FREEZE

▸▸ Suffered punishment/rejection for asserting themselves.

▸▸ May be 'taken captive' by abusive fight types/subject to domestic violence.

▸▸ May be convinced to stay in abusive relationships when the abuser love bombs them or charms them.

FAWN-FLIGHT

▸▸ Escapes the pain of self-abandonment by taking care of everyone else.

▸▸ Can be obsessive-compulsive clean freaks and caregivers.

▸▸ Project their perfectionism onto others.

▸▸ Sees themselves as perfect, selfless caregivers.

Summary

Understanding your default survival style will help you to change it. It is not your fault that you have cycles of emotional dysregulation. This is normal; you are a beautiful human being, not a robot. Fluctuations are to be anticipated. It is being able to identify when your response to an input does not qualify as reasonable. If you fly off the handle when someone spills something, this is most likely a stored response to how you were treated or dealt with that has now become a default state. Your default style and default operating system is a result of automatic wiring. It is a conditioned response that is based on your life lived to date. Your childhood, how attuned your caregivers were, and the level to which your core needs were met all feed into the conditioning of your internal defence system. You can recondition your operating system by bringing consciousness to what your patterns are, how you think and feel, and why you feel and think the ways that you do. Your goal is to build your capacity so you can ride out the inevitable cycles of emotional dysregulation. You build capacity and increase your window of tolerance by using the multi-systems approach of PEMS hygiene. Healing does not mean you never have emotional dysregulation; healing means that you can manage the dysregulation with more ease and capacity, and you no longer get buried by the highs and lows, emotionally or mentally.

CHAPTER 8

Stop Self-Abandoning

*"One does not become enlightened by imagining figures of light,
but by making the darkness conscious. The latter procedure,
however, is disagreeable and therefore not popular."*

–Carl Jung

Self-abandoning becomes ingrained by the nice girl programming I introduced you to in Chapter 1. You learn to self-abandon by putting others' needs, desires, and wishes above your own. You self-abandon when you cannot properly emote or feel your feelings. When you have experienced a chronic denial of your feelings, you will have latent anger build up. This anger will bubble beneath the surface, creating a feedback loop and reactivity cycle. To stop the reactivity cycle, you need to re-embrace your relationship to anger.

The reactivity cycle is commonly known as triggers. It is the rumination cycle, the conversations in your head about what you WOULD have said that you have over and over again. The would've, should've, could've game that we voice over after a dissatisfying, interpersonal experience. The reactivity cycle feeds the internal defence system of your nervous system.

It fuels the pre-loaded data that runs on autopilot until you override the programs with nervous system healing. It is okay to be angry. In fact, true recovery and healing depend on you harnessing your anger towards the people, places, and things that hurt you or disrespected you. These experiences helped to install your inner critic. They've influenced what your inner voice says to you, how you judge yourself, and how you move through the world. You are allowed to be angry at the people, places, and things that fuel that inner judgement, dampening your light and impacting your ability to heal. You are allowed to remove those people, places, and things who are currently contributing to keeping that inner critic alive. Use your anger to stop this inner critic in her tracks! By allowing yourself to be angry, you break the nice girl programming and stop self-abandoning.

You are allowed to use phrases like:

- *No*
- *Stop*
- *Shut up*
- *Fuck off*
- *You are not welcome here*

In fact, use these phrases every time you notice the run-away train of the inner critic. When you start to loop or move into circular thinking patterns, say "NO" to yourself! Practice saying these phrases to yourself whenever you become aware that you are in a reactivity cycle. I go so far as to imagine seeing a big, red stop sign in my mind when I recognize the loop starting up in my psyche. Using these phrases is a form of verbal ventilation, a vocal representation of a boundary, and a pattern interrupter! Verbal ventilation can short-circuit the hardwired negativity bias. This negativity bias has the potential of morphing into the inner prosecutor, the inner judge, the inner critic, habits of perfectionism, or a dramatization circuit that keeps you dysregulated. When you say "No" or use one of the other phrases, this conscious use of anger sets up an internal boundary that fortifies your sense of self and re-establishes your instincts of self-protection. It takes repetitive, consistent practice to dismantle the internal attacks from the inner critic. This is why implementing your own PEMS hygiene routine is so profound for self-protection and healing. The unconscious is more powerful than your conscious mind.

The *shadow* is a term Carl Jung coined to describe the unconscious parts of yourself that you repress. These parts need to be brought to light for your healing. The shadows are aspects of yourself that will be triggered through conflict and confrontation. Healing the shadow means confronting the aspects of your personality that you willfully ignore. Your shadow and your unconscious are synonymous; I will use them interchangeably for the purpose of this chapter, which is to teach you that it is okay to be angry. This book has been teaching you many ways to make friends with your shadow, giving you tools and techniques to dislodge the somatic sludge that forms a protective layer around your feelings, thoughts, and fears. It is okay that you choose to ignore the seemingly unpalatable or less desirable aspects of yourself. WE ALL DO! It is our human condition. But healing from the inside out means you have the courage to unveil those hidden, dark aspects. The shadow ties into that 'nice girl' programming, duping you into feigning interest or giving your energy away to harmful people, places, and things. By exploring your emotions, you discover your shadow; you unveil your unconscious. To do this practice, you have to go into your emotions. You have to feel your fucking feelings. This is scary, dear heart; I get that. The simplest way is the hardest way.

You have the intention to heal. You want to protect yourself and be the most stable, regulated version of yourself. How do I know you have this intention? Because you are reading this book! To marry that intention with outcomes means you need to be consistent. You need to treat this like a practice. Self-governance gets shut off through trauma. Recruiting your ability to interrupt a pattern is what helps you turn your self-governance back on. Pattern interrupting is how you will shift your consciousness.

Now, the next question is, how do you know what is conscious or unconscious? There is a part of you that is the observer, the part of you that knows you are reading this book. Your awareness knows you are in a room and that you are reading a book. Behind that observer are all the thoughts and feelings that make up your operating system. Those thoughts and feelings and emotions get kicked into gear when you receive a text from a certain someone as you are reading the book. The conscious parts of you know you are reading the book. The observer susses out what is happening in real time and what is happening based on your preloaded data in your operating system. The shadow and the unconscious make up parts of the pre-loaded data in your operating system and are logged into your autonomic nervous system. You are learning how to have a multi-point of awareness, growing and expanding from a single point of awareness. Your single point of awareness is most likely in survival mode.

Remember, trauma can be caused by the most benign things, as well as the really big things. Surgery, neglect, accidents, and abandonment (emotionally, physically, or mentally) all cause trauma. Trauma is a part of your shadow. Your shadow stuffs all the unhappy things caused by the little alarm systems that never get actualized in your body into a vault. Can't see your dog because he died when you were young, and no one explained where he went? Alarm system log activated. Parents shit all over an achievement, dismissing your accomplishments? Alarm system log activated. Cultivating your PEMS hygiene system dissipates that alarm system log. It starts with the intention to protect yourself better than anyone has ever protected you before! Then, identify the feelings by asking yourself how those people, places, and things make you feel. Then, you have to interrupt your default survival patterns (freeze, fight, flee, and fawn) by being present and feeling your feelings.

Writing down your angry feelings is a wonderful tool to feel the feelings, actualize the impulse, verbally ventilate, and get those unconscious, not-nice things you want to say out of your body! You can dislodge and clear undelivered communications out of your body-mind by writing what is affectionately dubbed "rage pages." Rage pages are solely for you to transmute the feelings out of your body-mind. This can help free you from the looping rumination of negative feelings or thoughts. Being able to mentally puke out your rage on a page is very cathartic. *You do not need to re-read these pages, and no one else gets to read them.* They do not need to even be coherent. This writing is to release the anger and rage that you have in your tissues/body from triggering inputs. You have to have a physical element, like writing on paper, not on your phone. It is the aspect of making something physical that makes this practice work. The kinesthetics of writing, of moving a pen or pencil on paper, help interrupt the patterns of circular thinking.

This is for the things that you would never say out loud. Being able to articulate them on a page is a form of verbal ventilation. You get to speak it in your mind (or out loud, in private) and then have a body connection through the act of writing on a page. Actualizing your feelings will help you clear out the trapped energy of an event or interaction. This clears the way to hear your gut intuition. It can inform your future self about people, places, and things that take you out of your flow.

To write a rage page, write out sentences after these prompts:

- *How fucking dare you...*
- *I can't believe you...*
- *The nerve you had...*
- *What the fuck do you think you are doing...*

After you choose one of the prompts to work with, you just let the mind and body say whatever it wants. As I mentioned, no one is going to read this; you don't even need to read it. Just move into an automatic writing mode and let it all flow out of you. Once you feel complete and there is no more to be said (for now), you can choose to throw it away or even burn the pages. I have a dedicated burn bowl on my patio for this very thing. Burning away the rage page is symbolic of the energy of rage as well as a very cleansing way to release the written rage. I use a simple clay bowl and an old pot lid to keep the fiery pages contained. After you are done with writing, it is important to rest for 8-12 minutes (or even longer if you need to or have extra time). Put on some music and lie down or sit quietly. This is training your nervous system to move from an activated place of anger to calmness. You are learning that it is safe to have anger and that you are allowed to express it in this safe manner. Rest is so often overlooked, but remember, your nervous system cannot be regulated without awareness and rest!

This is an intentional practice. Scrolling, watching TV, playing games, drawing, jiu-jitsu, etc., are activities. Activities that may help you self-soothe but do not adequately regulate the nervous system. This is where liminal space is important! Resting in the liminal space is KEY for regulation and, seriously, one of the hardest pieces to incorporate because, let's face it, it is scary to sit with our emotions. It is scary to just BE rather than DO. Resting in the liminal space helps prevent you from self-abandoning because you are being attentive to what you feel by feeling it. Sitting in it.

This will feel scary at first, learning how to sit with your feelings. Sitting with this fear is difficult but necessary. Meaning you will feel scared, but you will need to choose to do it anyway, learning that you can sit with the feelings without something terrible happening. By feeling the feelings, even when you are uncomfortable, you'll be able to recreate a sense of safety in your body. For example, saying the nasty things you want to say creates safety within.

Your autonomic nervous system creates chemicals and hormones when it feels scared and when it feels safe. Repatterning safety, stopping self-abandonment, and giving yourself a voice enables you to create new neural pathways and circuitry for you to travel down instead of suffering, misery, and pain. To rest and digest is critical, this is how your parasympathetic nervous system branch comes online. To rest and digest well, you have to live, rest, and get comfortable in liminal space. Movement and activity are wonderful distractions, but they can't replace resting in our feelings. Healing the nervous system is an intentional practice that you will get better at with practice.

So don't give up on yourself, dear heart. You cannot get it wrong when you have the intention to heal and regulate. Just showing up with the intention, and learning how to be rather than do, is the bulk of this work.

Now we need to talk about parents. Parents are the first humans you rely upon to have your core needs met. Unfortunately, there is a lot of opportunity for mismanagement and disorganization of your nervous system. Generational trauma is a thing, as your parents may come from their own line of PEMS hygiene defunct parents. Emotional intelligence is something that is learned, but many folks simply have not learned it. Many folks are emotionally immature, just playing at being adults. They pay bills and hold down jobs but do not know how to really feel or emote or communicate. It is more than likely that one or more of your core needs were not met in childhood.

Childhood trauma can develop from good parents, too. It doesn't always mean you suffered abuse or had bad parents. Childhood trauma means there were gaps between what you needed and what you got. It comes from not getting the love, support, and resources you needed, plain and simple. However well-intentioned your parents may have been, childhood trauma is a reality for most. Then, of course there are abusive parents. Peter Walker has this to say: "*Traumatizing parents cripple the instinctive fight response of their child, and recovering the anger of the fight response is essential to healing C-PTSD."*[17]

Writing your rage pages is a way for you to recover your anger. Try writing pages specific to your childhood and if this resonates for you, Peter Walker offers this script:

> *"Screw you, Mom and Dad, for frightening me*
> *so much about making mistakes that I freak*
> *out when things don't go peacefully."*

This is a gooder![18] Learning how to give yourself grace is paramount to your healing. As is radical self-acceptance. Overriding the initial inputs you learned as a child with patience, grace, flexibility, and kindness will help you shut down the inner critic. Can you see the pattern here on how to stop self-abandonment? It is by giving yourself permission to think the things you want, say what you need, and process your environment the way that serves you. When you stop self-abandoning you become present to your gut voice.

To stop self-abandoning, you make up the rules for how you interact with people, places, and things. You become attentive to how you communicate your core needs for love, trust, attunement, connection, and autonomy. Self-governance gets turned off by trauma, which means you have to deliberately turn it back on by thinking differently.

For example:

▶▶ You have a right to a process; you have a right to take steps and make mistakes. You do not have to achieve immediate perfection. This might not have been true when you were little, but it is true now.

---

[17]Pete Walker, (2013) *Complex PTSD: From Surviving to Thriving-A guide and map for recovering from childhood trauma,* Azure Coyote Publishing <Chapter 9-p. 179

[18] "Gooder" is Canadian slang for super good, something to keep, something to hold onto, something to celebrate.

▸ You have a right to how you see things, even if others don't see them the way you do. This may not have been true when you were little, but it is true now.

▸ The universe gave you a natural gut instinct, and now you are honouring it. That may not have been possible when you were growing up, but you are changing that now.

▸ You are allowed to be misunderstood. That may not have been true growing up, but it is true now.

▸ You are allowed to disagree. That might not have been allowed when you were growing up, but it is now.

These statements can be powerful affirmations, but I do not believe affirmations can work until you pinpoint what stored survival response gets activated. You will not believe an affirmation until your unmet core need has been acknowledged and soothed. Definitely spend time with rage pages before turning to affirmations. Spending time with the anger, rage, disappointment, fear, sadness, abandonment, and heartache you feel is what will help you shift it. It is how you stop self-abandoning. By feeling your feelings. By BEING and not DOING. You have to name it and claim it before you can release it. Name it to tame it. The purpose is to give your voice back to yourself, meet an aspect of one of your unmet core needs, or build upon the core needs being fulfilled. You are always in control of this healing, self-defence journey. Rage pages and specific journal prompts are part of your toolkit! Allowing yourself to say the nasty things (the critical self-judgement piece) removes the charge. If you can be with the shadow parts of yourself, they lose their power over you. By embracing the not nice parts you want to say, it clears the way for you to hear and receive the opposite.

Living between the excavation of stored survival responses and future self-dreaming is when you can use affirmations. Affirmations can be used to introduce or enforce a love language towards yourself, but they cannot heal the trauma from within alone. You must practice verbal ventilation, nervous system healing, somatic experiencing, and having healthy boundaries to protect yourself as you heal. This multi-directional approach is what the PEMS hygiene system is teaching you.

That being said, there is value in using affirmations as a love language to hear words that, perhaps, have never been introduced before. There is a 'fake it until you make it' attitude you can employ with this. You may feel silly at first, and you should definitely take notice of which affirmations below make you cringe or cause a reaction, as this could be indicative of a part of your shadow or unconscious self that needs healing. I have used affirmations for decades. It wasn't until I actively healed my nervous system that the affirmations landed differently. I can now feel and accept the phrases below. As with all the tools here, play with what lands for you and leave the rest. Be inquisitive and curious when you get a gut punch around the phrases and ask yourself, "Is this my instinct or a past trauma/ stored survival response making noise?"

Read through these and see which ones land for you:

- ▸▸ I deserve to be comfortable.
- ▸▸ I am allowed to be safe.
- ▸▸ I deserve to be pain-free.
- ▸▸ I have resources and support from safe, healthy people in my life.
- ▸▸ I will not allow inner or outer critics to attack or hold me hostage with their bullshit.
- ▸▸ I deserve to be happy.
- ▸▸ This is a temporary situation; it will not last forever.
- ▸▸ I deserve a loving relationship if I choose.
- ▸▸ I always have choices and options.
- ▸▸ I am allowed to make wise, loving, and good decisions for myself.

- ▸▸ I deserve boundless joy.

- ▸▸ I deserve a fulfilling and meaningful career.

- ▸▸ I deserve a support system.

- ▸▸ I can always reach out to someone safe in life to be heard, witnessed, and validated in any way that feels safe to me.

- ▸▸ I deserve to be acknowledged and honoured because all of my feelings are valid and deserve to be met with loving kindness, generosity, and self-acceptance.

- ▸▸ I have tools in my PEMS toolbox that allow me to self-soothe and comfort myself when I get dysregulated. There is no shame in feeling dysregulated because if you had had loving, attuned caregivers, you would not struggle in this way. It is okay that you are learning to do that now for yourself. In fact, it is a beautiful act of self-love for all the abandoned parts of yourself.

- ▸▸ I use my self-defence as self-care, like a total badass! Even when I make an unhealthy or misguided choice while I am dysregulated or feeling emotionally distressed.

- ▸▸ I deserve fun and play.

- ▸▸ I deserve good friends.

- ▸▸ I deserve vibrant health.

- ▸▸ I deserve to have all my needs met.

Consider choosing one phrase to say every day for a week and then swap it out with another one. Personally, I use the simplest greeting as a love language for myself. Every night and every morning, I say, "I love you, Diane," three times. I have been doing this for the past four years, and it is the most reassuring way to start and end my days. The shocking truth is that you have to train yourself to feel good! The negativity bias, coupled with the shadow and inner critic, means you are habitually pulled towards the negative. You are not bad or broken when you focus on the negative. You are human. To train yourself to stop self-abandoning, you will need to self-soothe through verbal ventilation and your social engagement system and then practice positive noticing.

Positive noticing is reinforcing positive behaviour by noticing when you do good things, have positive traits, and have positive accomplishments. This will feel super foreign when you start. Putting in the work requires radical honesty, discipline, courage, and consistency. Do not reject these tools because they seem simple. What you say you will do and what you actually do need to be aligned for this to work.

You are worth it, dear heart! You deserve to be fiercely protected and celebrated! I talk about this being hard work, but healing and feeling better is actually fun. Clearing out energy and releasing undelivered communications will give you strength. These practices will empower you to protect your personal safety and fortify the boundaries you need for your peace of mind. If you put in the repetitions, like you would if you were perfecting a recipe, training for a marathon, or learning your lines for a presentation, you will reap the benefits.

These practices move you from a single point of awareness (being stuck in survival mode) into a multi-point awareness. This is how you re-learn how to feel safe in your body-mind. You create the environment for yourself from within. The only reason people don't heal is because they didn't know they could or because they never tried. I really believe this to be true. Your body ALWAYS wants optimal well-being; you just need to have the courage and support to sit with what you got. Then, as best you can, create opportunities to revisit yourself. Over and over again. Gently. Healing is not about perfection. Healing does not mean you are totally contained or calm. When I talk about healing what I mean is the opposite of the oppressive traits of trauma that cause major hangups and hiccups in your life. Healing is having an expanded window of tolerance to be able to tolerate more significant situations with people, places, and things more consistently. Healing is experiencing life outside of survival mode.

CHAPTER 9

Cultivate Your Awareness

Awareness is one of the three pillars of practicing self-defence, along with Avoidance and Attitude. Cultivating self-awareness can go by many names: practicing mindfulness, awarenessing, becoming alert, being tuned in, or growing your attentiveness. Self-awareness is even linked to consciousness itself. But awareness is not a by-product of consciousness; it is a learned skill. Awareness of people, places, and things is how you have a safety state of mind. You need to know who has access to you at all times. You need to be aware of when the energy shifts in a public space and when someone's behaviour or face/mood changes. Awareness means you are gathering information to make decisions. Should you stay? Are you safe? Is there a better spot? Where is help? Troubleshooting these types of questions is what having awareness looks like as you move through the world.

When you take the PEMS hygiene approach, you set yourself up for a whole-body awareness routine. Continually using a PEMS hygiene routine will enable you to distinguish when the past interrupts the present, meaning that with awareness, you always have an opportunity to re-organize your internal defence system. Bringing awareness to your physical, emotional, mental, and spiritual self allows your own healing.

You can restructure how you interpret the inputs you receive from people, places, and things and change your neural pathways. That is the power of awareness and PEMS training.

Self-awareness is the ability to know what you are doing, when you are doing it, and why you are doing it! This takes skill! We are prone to moving through life on autopilot. Earning a living, raising kids, advancing in our careers, healing, and just being in the world is hard work. Human nature dictates that to cope with the demands of life, we automate certain things, like the route we drive home or the order at the restaurant. You are not bad or broken for using automation. We all do it. The magic sauce is recognizing when you do it and then interrupting that pattern so you can be present to the world around you.

By using the tools and techniques in this book, you can improve your awareness. Whenever you take time to discern how you feel in the present moment and why you feel what you feel or what you have felt in the past, you build up your awareness muscle. Without self-awareness, your thoughts, feelings, and personal behaviour patterns are controlled by unconscious beliefs and assumptions. These unconscious beliefs can drive the automation, the tuning out, and the gut reaction to inputs that may not be accurate. Without self-awareness, it is difficult to trust your intuition because you can't distinguish your own internal voice from the noise around you. If you don't know where you end and someone else begins, that can become dangersome.[19]

Dangersome is just like it sounds: dangerous, perilous, and inadvisable. If you do not know where you begin and end, your sense of self easily becomes enmeshed with those around you. You will take on energy, responsibilities, and duties that do not originate from you and create

---

[19]This is a word that the fictional character, Moira Rose, uses in the TV show *Schitt's Creek*. This show and her character continue to be a tool for soothing my nervous system. Re-watching a show or movie that you enjoy creates a safe, predictable experience that can have a calming effect. This re-watching is a valuable form of self-care and a wonderful nervous system regulation technique. Being able to safely self-soothe is the opposite of dangersome.

even more distance from being able to hear your gut instincts. It is dangersome to make others' needs a priority over your own. It is dangersome to let others' opinions be louder than your own. You need to be able to hear your gut instincts to have a safety state of mind. Those gut instincts act as a subconscious alarm system that understands people, places, and things on an energy level. You need awareness so you can feel and hear when those alarm bells fire off. Re-calibrating how to listen to your gut instincts is done by separating your conditioned patterns from past experiences to trusting how to embody the present moment and the cues therein. Gavin Becker, from the book *The Gift of Fear,*[20] writes, "*Intuition connects us to the natural world and to our nature. Freed from the bonds of judgement, married only to perception, it carries us to predictions we will later marvel at!*" Your gut punch can tell the future when you know how to listen to it. You learn how to trust your gut punch when you begin to heal your trauma.

Self-awareness enables you to understand your behaviours, habits, personality, motivations, emotional reactions, and thought processes so much better. A lack of self-awareness can create pain and suffering because of the unconscious programs (the preloaded data in your nervous system) that are activated or triggered by people, places, and things. Becoming aware of your boundaries and your value system, as well as appreciating what core needs have been disrupted, will help you release stored survival responses. Then, you can re-organize your internal language and re-establish your connection to self, using self-defence from the inside out! This is how you cultivate self-awareness. Then, you will be able to hone your intuition and re-awaken your gut instincts. You can make better choices when you have self-awareness.

The easiest thing to do when you want to build your awareness is to ground yourself in your immediate space. Ask yourself what you can see, hear, feel, touch. This helps pull your consciousness into the moment

---

[20] Gavin de Becker, 1997, *The Gift of Fear*, Little, Brown and Company

and can be used to override anxious rumination and racing thoughts. Get into the habit of anchoring your consciousness daily by checking in with what you can see, hear, touch, and feel. Remember it is simple repetition that builds skills.

Questions to Ask Yourself That Improve Self-Awareness:

When do I feel happy?

How do I know if I am sad?

What makes me angry?

What am I afraid of?

When do I feel my body get tired?

How do I know what my feelings are?

Can I feel the difference between fear and ecstasy?

Why do I ignore my gut instincts?

When do I push through?

When do I pull in?

Why did I agree to _____?

Can I give myself permission to stay at home?

What does my little, inside voice say about certain people, places, and things?

How often do I ignore that inside voice?

What does reading these questions make me feel?

How often do I criticize myself when I am learning something new?

When am I kind and nice to myself?

Where do I give myself the benefit of the doubt?

When do I let myself off the hook?

How can I be gentler in my mind towards myself?

Those questions you just read are not an opportunity for Judge Judy to show up. This is an exercise in contemplation. They are for you to become aware of the feelings and sensations that dictate how you move through your day. I want you to consider how you can make changes so that you move through life feeling safe and supported from within. The more self-awareness you can cultivate, the more protection you will be able to offer yourself!! How many times has your mind been swimming in the maze of rehashed conversations or future worries, and you get home not remembering the route you took? You were on autopilot and got from A to B without any awareness because you were consumed by your own mind and stress. These moments are worth your recognition. You need to realize that your busy mind is too full and that your body-mind connection needs to be reestablished.

When you live with chronic, low-grade stress, your nervous system can get stuck in fight or flight mode. This is akin to having your foot on the brake and gas at the same time. The natural survival instinct gets stuck in hyperdrive, never really turning off. This survival state that is meant to alert you of danger is now popping off when you have to return a phone call or answer an email. This constant state of stress, below the veil of consciousness, will consistently dump stress hormones, causing physiological changes in your body that can lead to heart disease, high blood pressure, anxiety, and depression. Without awareness, you will misread cues and judge life experiences from an activated state of being.

Your mind is your greatest weapon in self-defence!

If you have a high ACE[21] score and grew up in a turbulent family system, you may have become used to living with high levels of stress. Chaos may feel familiar and read as safety to you if that was your experience growing up. The high stress and volatility will become a learned input. Without awareness, you will continue to seek out chaos because it was a natural environment that informed your internal defence system growing up. Choosing to practice awareness is self-care. *Awareness is self-protection.*

Learning how to say no, ask for help, outsource jobs, decline invitations, and make yourself a priority is awarenessing. You are allowed to learn a new state of being that provides safety and calmness and injects peaceful existence into your internal defence system. You are allowed to just BE and not always have to DO! It just takes practice. Practice giving yourself permission to rewrite your story. Practice sensing the environment you choose to live in. Always remember that cultivating awareness will fortify your intuition, build a safety state of mind, and cultivate the art of self-protection instincts. Your mind is your greatest weapon in self-defence!

Cultivating awareness and building intuition are achieved with consistent, actionable steps. These steps are continually refined and engaged as you move along the timeline of life. Ask yourself what you are doing, when you are doing it, and why you are doing it! Determine what your boundaries are. Develop and nurture your own value system. Protect your peace of mind and choose people, places, and things that contribute to your peace.

---

[21] Adverse Childhood Experiences. If you want to know yours, check-out: https://traumadissociation.com/ace

Tips to Cultivate Awareness

▶▶ Learn how to be comfortable in liminal space, free of stimulation. Try to expand in liminal space by not reaching for your phone right when you wake up, and instead, take some time to just BE. This is hard, I know. We are so conditioned to be constantly entertained, to always be busy, to constantly be searching, scrolling, or updating. We're told we always need to be engaged. Delaying looking at your phone an hour on each side of going to bed or getting up helps the brain be comfortable in the in-between, liminal space. When we're free from distractions, living in the liminal space builds awareness.

▶▶ Rest is paramount for the body-mind to learn how to listen to itself.

▶▶ Using guided meditations and practicing mindfulness builds your intuition.

▶▶ Create a space that you can be mindful in, like a meditation corner, or have a few items like crystals or candles you bring out when you wish to have a mindful session of awarenessing.

▶▶ Creating a ritual of clearing a space (this can be a counter or desktop) by placing treasured, meaningful items on it triggers the mind for the space you are cultivating. The space of YOU!

▶▶ Try to do the recapitulation exercise (see Chapter 18) once a month or every quarter. This exercise will free up lost energy and help you to reclaim your power from triggering inputs.

▶▶ Dance, play, go on the swing set, jump on a trampoline, and get into your body! Losing our sense of play and wonderment hampers our self-awareness and intuition, so resurrect playful elements in your life!

In our culture of quick fixes and immediate gratification, we have all emboldened the concept of biohacking. We all covet the fast track! In healing and self-defence there isn't one; there is no fast track. But honing awareness, mastering personal protection strategies, and regulating your nervous system is as close as you will get to a bio-hack. Learn how to hack your internal defence system.

That is what will create change.

CHAPTER 10

Attitude—Fake It Until You Make It

Have you heard of the ol' axiom "fake it until you make it?" Would it surprise you to also know that this works for self-defence? Confidence training is a form of self-defence because it reinforces an attitude that can deflect predators and other people, places, and things that want to do harm. This attitude training helps you build your self-esteem, and it can rewire your brain.[22]

In fact, a new breakthrough in neuroscience has revealed that self-confidence can now be directly amplified in the brain. Not only can confidence be improved regardless of skill levels improving, but the participants were able to maintain the new levels of confidence. Dr. Hakwan Lau, Associate Professor in the UCLA Psychology Department and senior author on this study, said, "Crucially, in this study, confidence was measured quantitatively via rigorous psychophysics, making sure the effects were not just a change of mood or simple reporting strategy. Such changes in confidence took place even though the participants performed the relevant tasks at the same performance level."

---

[22]ScienceDaily, 15 December 2016. www.sciencedaily.com/releases/2016/12/161215085902.htm

Attitude is one of the three pillars of creating a safety state of mind.

Attitude is one of the three pillars of creating a safety state of mind. Being able to convey the right attitude to dissuade people from taking advantage of you is one of the foundational principles in my self-defence program.

Faking it 'till you make it is important because confidence, self-assurance, and feeling safe to take up space are not readily accessible to women. The sad truth of it is that repressing women is a national pastime that is bred into the fabric of society. There are so many cultural, familial, and societal pressures that undermine a woman's self-esteem, her worth, and her value. Nice girl programming and the patriarchy will wreak havoc on your confidence. Faking it until you make it is a suit of armour you can put on, using a mantra, a good outfit, a hat, carrying a totem (like a rock, crystal, or knife) that will level you up and portray an attitude of confidence, even when your feelings may be reticent.

Why do high-achieving women teach the power pose? Because it changes how we behave. What is the power pose? It is standing up tall, feet a little wider than your hips, making a fist in both hands, placing those fisted hands on your hips, chin up, eyes bright, taking in the world around you. Picture Wonder Woman! Try this right now: Strike a power pose and even give yourself Wonder Woman bracelets in your mind as you do the power pose. The power pose will summon energy and confidence, even when you don't feel it initially. Employing body language that is strong, steady, and determined allows us to adopt a feeling of agency and self-possession. The sense of agency and bodily autonomy that may have been siphoned out of you, knowingly or unknowingly, over time. If you have had your power taken away from you or repeatedly had your boundaries disrespected, demonstrating power-pose body language and claiming a boundary can feel like a betrayal. This is okay. That feeling of betrayal comes from an old pattern that took power away from you and taught you that you could not have agency. You can change that pattern by faking it until you make it. It gets easier, trust me. At first, you may feel a bit silly, standing like Wonder Woman, saying nice things to yourself. Then it gets easier because a deep part of you will recognize this state of autonomy, this agency that is a God-given right.

Think back to the confidence we had as little girls in our fairy dresses, butterfly wings, and Batman masks, riding our bikes and heading to the grocery store with our Grandma. There will be pieces of freedom that you can recollect from when you were young and free. The time before life dampened your light and affected your attitude.

My client, Mary, is an author, suffers from chronic illness and works from home. She has more bad days than good when it comes to her work output. But she is a total baller when it comes to personal growth and personal protection strategies. One of her favourite life hacks to feel confident is to put on red lipstick. Mary will put a clip in her hair and apply red lipstick, and this will trigger her brain to activate the output mode she wishes to emulate. She becomes more confident in her attitude because of this lipstick. This is faking it until you make it. She told me a story of a particularly bad night of major colitis. She was on the loo for hours and hours, contemplating this "Am I going to die?" internal monologue that creeps into her mind every month due to the severity of her illness. Mary had a Zoom call with her publisher in six minutes. Looking into the mirror, she could see that her outside matched her inside. Tired, overwrought, circles under eyes, greyish skin tone. She got into her fake it until you make it mindset and took action: She washed her face, spritzed fragrance for the bathroom and her body, applied a liberal application of cherry red lipstick, put in some hair gel, added a bobby pin for the side part, donned a great sweater with the perfect cowl neck, and voila! Her armour was on. She completed her mini-ritual for confidence and had a minute to spare to set up her computer. Mary was ready for the Zoom. Her outsides masked her insides as she began, but once complete, she could feel stamina return. The mask worked to bring her up and out of the tired, haggard state. Her intention to harness some confidence worked, her attitude shifted, and she was able to show up for life in that moment.

Our minds can change our bodies.
Our bodies can change our minds.
Our behaviour changes the outcome.

Confidence comes from the inside out and the outside in.

Confidence does not come from achievement per se; it comes from your internal belief that you are good, worthy, and deserving. Confidence comes from the inside out and the outside in, which is great news because it means you can be better at it! You can learn to be confident. By pivoting away from programmed beliefs that you are not worth it, these one-degree shifts will change your attitude with practice. You get to decide to be confident like Mary did.

Now, I know this may sound silly or even trigger some derogatory baggage that putting on lipstick may evoke. I get it. The beauty industry has been weaponized against women, taking shots at our appearance and beguiling us with products that are not needed. Yet, it worked for Mary, and it even works for me. Lip colour will brighten your face and can lend us a brightness that we may not feel. That brightness can make us feel more confident and shift our attitude. That is all. I believe in natural beauty. No woman needs makeup, but it can be a tool.

How people perceive you will determine how they interact with you. From a self-defence point of view, appearing confident reduces being perceived as a victim. The best way to appear confident is to adopt a good posture. A good posture is achieved with your stance, having a balanced gait, and being aware of your surroundings. Good posture shows the world that you are ready, engaged, anticipatory, and present. Bullies and predators target weak, uncertain women. Please note: There is NEVER an intention to victim shame. YOU never deserve someone hurting you! However, having the wrong posture can make the difference between an assailant or predator seeing you as a target or as a passerby. Why? Because your posture, body language, and other non-verbals communicate information. We infer information from non-verbal communication and body language. Adopting a posture that infers comfortable confidence as opposed to shy submissiveness is a marked difference. How you choose to be seen in the world is an important decision in self-defence.

Nonverbals govern how others see us, but they also govern how we see ourselves. Think about how you feel when you put on your favourite outfit and go out in the world as opposed to when you are in a slouchy sweatpants mood. You can feel the difference between when you want to be seen and when you don't. Posture can be thought of as how you carry yourself. Head up, eyes tracking your environment, watching the space around you, registering your surroundings, confident and present. Practicing a safety state of mind is making sure you convey an attitude of confidence and self-assuredness when you are out and about.

In my self-defence program, I teach the phrase, "Don't Be a Victim." This in no way implies that your actions can be used to justify an attack. Nor does it mean that you deserve an assault because you look like a victim. Rather, it is a phrase that snaps you into awareness. Predators look for women/girls who are distracted, dishevelled, stand with rounded shoulders, have an unsteady gait, and keep their eyes cast down, looking like they want to disappear. A predator wants someone they can easily overtake. Why? Because predators are usually cowards who want an easy target. They want to overpower and intimidate, so they specifically look for girls/women who they think won't put up a fight, and they infer that information by the body language and attitude that you convey. Having good posture is a basic self-defence principle that requires no extra skill or advanced training. Good posture equals a confident attitude.

How you enter a room, walk down the street, stand at the bus stop, and carry yourself in a crowd all matter when it comes to self-defence. We all have cell phones these days, and we are likely using them in public, especially when we are alone. Having our heads down, engulfed in our cell phones, has to be interspersed with looking up and around, always clocking what is happening around us. It's the simple act of looking up when someone new gets on the bus or enters the vicinity that you occupy. Learn how to take notice.

I know what it is like when you feel uncomfortable by unwanted attention from someone who makes your alarm bells ring. You want to shrink from view. You look away. You look down. You think if you avoid them, they will leave you alone. This is incorrect. The best thing to do is to make eye contact, stand up straight, and be comfortable and ready in your body. You are not puffing up your chest like a peacock or staring with aggression, but you need to have good posture and a strong stance. It really can be that simple: looking confident, aware, and ready. This is cultivating a safety state of mind with your attitude.

Fake it till you make it!

Attitude and confidence is a state of mind. By choosing how you think, act, and behave in the present moment, you can cultivate and radiate an attitude of confidence. Do not be worried if this feels fake at first. Remember: Fake it till you make it! Over time, you will build a new neural network that responds to inputs that develop and increase your confidence. Adopting this practice of faking it until you make it works in real time; the more you practice it, the easier it gets, and the more neural pathways are created that support this attitude.

Here are three techniques broken down for you to use to cultivate the attitude of confidence or to do your confidence training.

1. Stand Tall

Claim your space by standing tall. Drop your shoulders down away from your ears, straighten, and lift yourself up with your spine. Embody a safe, confident stance. Your feet should be a little more than shoulder-width apart. Your feet can create a V shape or, ideally, an L shape, where one foot is where you can escape to, and the other is pointed forward. Have equal weight on both the right and left leg. Slightly bend your knees so you are not rigid or locked in your stance. Drop your centre into your feet so you feel like you are in your legs.

2. Make Eye Contact

This shows you are aware of the people, places, and things around you. Being aware, responsive, and engaged is key to confidence training. Shifty eyes read as inattentive, scattered, or disorganized. 'Where your eyes go, your energy flows.' Practice by scanning the crowd, the restaurant, or those around you while waiting at the bus stop. Looking at the cashier or waiter in the eyes when being helped. Practice looking at yourself in the mirror and holding your own gaze. This also helps anticipate threats. To be able to anticipate a possible threat, you have to be able to read your surroundings. This starts with being able to hold your gaze and your focus. In the chapter on Situational Awareness, I cover threat cues and what to *look* for and be *aware* of. Harnessing the skill of being able to determine pre-incident behaviours, seeing what is around you, and being able to interpret and intention will help you as you build your confidence.

3. Show Your Hands

Body language says a lot about a person, so keeping your hands visible versus shoved into your pockets is a sign of confidence. It shows you are ready, aware, and receptive to your environment. Having the hands visible and using them in conversation also keeps you in the ready posture. Ready to thwart, redirect, intuit, or respond to something that comes at you. Having your hands up and out as opposed to crossed or hanging at the side of your body makes you appear more confident, and it is the safest place for them. Practice holding onto your purse strap or backpack, the lapels of a sweater, or even your hair. Keep your hands up and out in public.

These techniques and practices will boost your confidence. They give you a dopamine hit each time your consciousness comes back to them, so doing these practices will give you a sense of accomplishment. Feeling a sense of accomplishment is a great mood stabilizer, and you will find that having a confident attitude helps you feel protected.

CHAPTER 11

Avoidance—Staying Out of Trouble

My husband had a running joke in the dojo for years. It goes like this.

"How do you avoid being sucker punched in a biker bar?"
"Don't be in a biker bar!"

Avoiding dangerous or suspect people, places, and things is paramount to practicing self-defence. Learn how to listen to those gut instincts that convey information that the mind can barely put words to and avoid an action that you may potentially regret. The companion chapter for Avoidance is Situational Awareness, which breaks down what to avoid in specific situations. Avoidance is important because it can be a subtle and nuanced way to protect your peace of mind without letting others know your reasons. You never have to justify what actions you take to bring yourself peace of mind, provided those actions are ethical and non-violent, but that goes without saying. Avoiding people, places, and things that are dangerous should be obvious, and yet, we all somehow can override our instincts.

Here are ways you can avoid situations or people.

Avoid Draining People

Do you have that one friend or relative who, after you spend time with them, leaves you feeling drained? Practice avoiding them. You have my permission. Learning how to avoid people who drain your energy, waste your time, and do not enhance your quality of life is allowed.

Have you had consistent phone calls with an associate that depletes you and expends what little energy you have left in the day? Try to avoid exposure to those interactions. You are allowed to have boundaries around work colleagues, family, friends, and associates.

You have permission to break the cycle. Stop taking end-of-day phone calls or emails that rattle you and throw you into the future before you have a chance to finish with the day at hand.

Avoid getting into a car or being in an enclosed space with someone who is unknown to you. This could be not sharing an Uber with a mutual acquaintance that abruptly happens because all your friends have already left in another car. Excuse yourself to go back inside, say you have to make a phone call and check in on your aunt, and give yourself permission to decline out of convenience or wanting to be nice. Train yourself to pause, think, assess, and re-assess.

Avoid Rushing Into Dating

New romances deserve your time and consideration. A dynamic spark and whirlwind romance that takes your breath away but is hard to define, or that overwhelms you, could actually be an unhealthy connection or even a trauma bond. A trauma bond is an intense emotional attachment that develops between two people within a toxic, abusive, or exploitative relationship. It can happen quite quickly between a predatory, toxic person and someone yearning to be loved and understood. There is a cycle of abuse and positive reinforcement. It is the attachment to an abuser that is hard to break or define because of the intermittent reinforcement of love, expressions of regret, profession of changed behaviour, and grand gestures after mistreatment or abuse. The abuser makes you feel safe and connected after the abuse cycle, so it is tremendously confusing and overwhelming. In fact, you can develop a chemical, neurological addiction to the cycle that defies reason and makes it exceptionally hard to leave or break up. There is a legit feedback loop that is created with hormones and dopamine kicks that form in a trauma bond. Knowing how to avoid these people is important, and it takes a bit of learning how to spot the red flags.

A red flag in a new relationship is the new person being overly familiar with you, showing up uninvited, or giving your grand gifts right out of the gate. A red flag would be them rationalizing their bad behaviour and defending their poor communication. Controlling speech or behavior that they may try to laugh off equals a red flag. I give more examples in the chapter on Predatory Behaviour.

A trauma bond can mimic a familiar sense of danger that is logged in your internal defence system based on your family system. What you think is love at first sight could actually be a subconscious recognition of the same kind of chaos you grew up with, so this new somebody will feel familiar and safe based on your past experiences. Without doing the excavation into nervous system healing and upgrading the software of your internal defence system, old patterns will play out, even if they are unhealthy. Do not avoid potential red flags in favour of excitement. And most importantly, learn the difference between trauma bonds, pattern recognition or denial, red flags, and healthy connection styles.

Pattern recognition is seeing the patterns you choose, the patterns in your behavioral style, and the behavior you choose in others. You can spot good patterns and bad patterns. If you readily dismiss poor behavior when you are first dating someone, this is an example of denying your pattern recognition. A healthy connection is based on mutual respect, kindness, and a desire to positively contribute to one another's lives. On the other hand, in a trauma-bonded relationship, you will act out of guilt, manipulation, fear, and obligation. A healthy connection can resolve conflict with productive methods that strengthen the relationship and are collaborative. In a trauma bond, conflict is avoided in favour of coercion, and discussion episodes escalate as the toxic member (s) of the relationship attempt to gain control of the dialogue and cause the other person to become dependent on them. Understanding your nervous system baseline is crucial to understanding what inputs you respond to. I grew up with excessive violence and rarely felt safe. I did high-adrenaline sports to replicate the feeling of danger that was inputted into my nervous system from a young age. I was in a trauma-bonded relationship. My own nervous system blueprint had me ever so comfortable with danger and codependency to toxic relationships. That was a learned behaviour that informed my nervous system from a young age. I had to learn how to be content without drama. I had to recalibrate so I could feel satisfied and calm. I had to relearn what safe, secure, love felt like. When I learned what to avoid in my life so I could have my core needs met, my life started to thrive!

- ▸▸ Do you feel dissatisfied without a degree of tension in your life?

- ▸▸ Do you notice that you cannot avoid picking apart conversations, relationships, or experiences you have in your life?

These are all indicative of how well your core needs are being met (or not met), what you need to avoid in your life, and what you can re-organize so you, too, can relearn what safety feels like.

- ▸▸ Is being calm a vegetative state for you, like binge-watching a show or tuning out completely?

▶▶ Can you be calm and alert? Calm and satisfied?

▶▶ Do you avoid conflict because you hate difficult conversations?

Avoidance needs to be treated like a skill. When you can skillfully employ avoidance of not just dangerous things but energy-sucking people, places, and things, you will be practicing good self-defence from the inside out. Avoiding self-inquiry into what makes you tick will not help you. The only way out is through. Taking the time to read this book is already re-calibrating your courage to re-organize and establish a connection with your core needs. Reading these concepts and techniques introduces options into your internal defence system that you can develop and acquire competency in. You have the time and the resources to avoid people, places, and things that are harmful to your PEMS hygiene system.

My student Lucy has a tricky relationship with her sister. Her sister dominates her energy and her time. Her sister makes certain that her life, her needs, her desires, and her caretaking are the priority in the relationship. It is difficult to witness the exchange of strong narcissistic tendencies with boundary-less codependency. Small, bite-sized pieces of avoidance are helping Lucy re-create balance.

For starters, Lucy has learned to avoid taking her sister's phone calls multiple times a day and to voice when she is upset or feeling overwhelmed by her sister's demands. She is learning that it is safe to have boundaries with her sister. It is a practice that takes tremendous strength, as the family dynamic is very well established. When Lucy shifts the focus back to her own wants, needs, and desires, she becomes motivated to safeguard her time and energy.

Another student of mine, Gale, has an ex that dictates when and how he will show up as a co-parent. She has had to learn how to avoid the fawning response that makes her compliant, allowing him to be in control all the time. This fawning response is an emotional behavioural response that can show up as a form of shutdown or immobilization.

The fawning response is the ultimate avoidance tactic of our internal defence system, and though it is excellent when faced with someone who exhibits violence, it is not ideal as a coping mechanism to avoid having boundaries.

Gale would shut down because she didn't feel safe having needs with her ex. He made it obvious that his financial support relied on his dominant connection style and her compliance, so Gale avoided communicating with him for fear of losing financial support. Gale recognized that she was avoiding having necessary conversations with him about co-parenting, which caused great resentment and unease in her life. She was stressed out, thinking that if she voiced a boundary or a need, he would withdraw all support. She realized that this was incredibly unhealthy and unbalanced. Avoiding the conversation meant she would continue to feel stressed and lose energy, self-esteem, and patience. She started small by not answering the last-minute requests for time and declining the impromptu events that he wanted her and her daughter to show up for. Avoiding the default behaviour that can develop when there is a power imbalance helped Gale to establish a co-parenting routine. When you practice self-awareness, you will see what patterns you perpetuate and whether or not those patterns serve your well-being. From that awareness, you learn how to avoid people, places, and things that cause you harm, whether physically, emotionally, spiritually, or mentally.

Avoid Overextending Yourself!

Something occurred to me recently when I was laid up with a sickness and had very low energy. On day three or four of convalescing, I had to go out and get a few chores done. When I left the house, I realized how vulnerable, wounded, and insular I felt because of the flu that was plundering my resources. This vulnerability made me feel uncomfortable in my body in a self-defence scenario, and I chose to go home and reach out to friends to bring me the items I was initially set to go get myself.

The likelihood of having a confrontation was minimal, but we cannot foretell the future.

Knowing that I was not able to focus on awareness outside of my own achy body, the smart thing to do was avoid my exposure to any undue stress. This is practicing self-defence, knowing your limits, respecting your own boundaries, and avoiding scenarios that are unnecessary. Be discerning in your choices and know how and when you have energy for output. Too often, women simply muscle through tasks and put themselves at the end of the receiving line. We say things like, "I will rest once 'x,y,z' is accomplished." But you need to realize that doing x,y,z is at the expense of your emotional, mental, spiritual, and physical well-being.

I encourage you to stay safe every day. This applies when we are under stress, too. Whether it is an overwhelming social calendar, a new job, or family commitments, being burdened by external expectations can cause you to become overextended. Being overextended then causes stress, and stress will take you off your centre. Practice listening to your own needs, and do not place external challenges on yourself when you are low on energy or output.

Your new mantra is: "If I am not at my best, I will rest."

What if you cannot reschedule? Reach out to friends and family to come with you so you avoid being alone. This could be asking a friend to go grocery shopping with you, a colleague to go to the library with you, or a family member to take you to an appointment. Communicate with your trusted tribe and let them know when you are having a hard time. People love to be useful and lend a hand to those they care about.

If I am not at my best, I will rest.

Avoiding difficult people, places, and things can feel foreign and tricky at the start. If you have had your boundaries hammered on and grew up without your voice being heard, setting a boundary or a need will feel uncomfortable. More than that, setting a boundary can feel like self-betrayal if you were conditioned *not* to have any boundaries growing up. That's why up next is a whole chapter on learning healthy boundaries to help you choose what you say no to and what you say yes to.

Take solace, dear heart; it will get easier the more you do it!

CHAPTER 12

Healthy Boundaries 101

*"Your life story is shaped by what you
say yes to and what you say no to"*

–Sarri Gilman

I will be the first to admit that no one taught me how to have boundaries, and I was miserable at them for many years. In fact, it was dangerous to speak out in my family. Women and girls weren't supposed to have an opinion. I was taught to go along to get along, put others' needs before mine, not to make a fuss or have needs, be seen and not heard, be useful, and not seek attention. I would venture a guess and say no one taught you how to have healthy boundaries, either. Rest assured, having healthy boundaries is a skill that you can learn, and this chapter is a start to that.

Having healthy boundaries means:

▸▸ you can say no without feeling guilty.

▸▸ you can ask for what you need or want.

▸▸ you do things out of desire/interest as opposed to obligation.

▸▸ you behave according to your own values and beliefs.

In short, having good boundaries means you can stand up for yourself! Learning how to stand up for yourself can feel really weird and uncomfortable if you were programmed to ignore your needs. Please know it is natural to feel these things and that it gets better with practice! You are indeed worthy of having healthy boundaries. What you think, how you feel, and what you want matters! In self-defence, we use boundaries because boundaries keep you safe! Boundaries define where you end and someone else begins. Having good boundaries is a mental practice as well as a physical one. Physical boundaries protect your space and your body! Learning how to simply put your hand up when someone unknown approaches you to ask their intent is an example of practicing a physical boundary.

Choosing who has a right to touch you, asking for privacy, and communicating your body's needs for rest and nourishment are examples of physical boundaries. Having boundaries keeps you safe and tells others what is acceptable when they wish to interact with you! You have a right to decide who has access to your body, to your mind, and to your soul. Boundaries can define what you value, what you stand for, how you wish to be treated, and what behaviour you expect from others if they want access to you.

> *Boundaries determine what you say*
> *"Yes" to and what you say "No" to.*

I want you to be able to say yes to the things that replenish you. Say yes to being supported, feeling safe to disagree, and expressing your difficult emotions. I want you to devote some energy to knowing who you are, what you want, what lights you up, and what you really feel.

I want you to learn how to say no to people, places, and things that drain your energy. Say no to taking on other people's responsibilities, say no to the guilt that crops up when you make yourself a priority, and say no to the bullshit belief that taking care of your needs/values/wants is selfish.

Being able to say no is actually a very loving thing to do. It teaches others how they need to treat you, and it empowers those close to you to do the same!

The biggest obstacle to having healthy boundaries is fear! Fear of conflict, fear of disappointing people, fear of rejection, and fear of abandonment will all creep in when you start practicing this new skill.

We all want to feel loved and accepted.

We all want to feel safe.

We all want some measure of control.

These are root programs installed into each and every one of us. Learning something new and stepping outside your comfort zone will threaten these root programs to some degree, but only initially. Once you begin to feel safe making your wants and needs a priority, the new, weird, uncomfortable feelings begin to subside. You will actually start to feel more powerful, more stable, and more in control. It is absolutely possible to feel safe and have healthy boundaries; it just takes practice!

Boundaries in a Healthy Relationship:[23]

+ Saying no without guilt.

+ Asking for what you want or need.

+ Taking care of yourself.

+ Doing things out of interest/desire, not out of obligation or to please others.

+ Behaving according to your own values and beliefs.

+ Feeling safe to express difficult emotions and also to disagree.

+ Feeling supported to pursue your goals.

---

[23] Courtesy of Sharon Martin, LCSW

✦ Being treated as an equal.

✦ Taking responsibility for your happiness and not feeling responsible for the happiness of someone else.

✦ Being in tune with your own feelings.

How Do You Set Healthy Boundaries?

It begins with a choice. Are you allowed to choose how people treat you? Do you know how to show people in your life what your boundaries are? Even if you don't feel a yes immediately, *the answer to both those questions is a yes.* It starts with mindset! You must first begin by choosing that you are worthy of having boundaries. Deciding to value what you feel, think, want, prefer, and need to feel safe is a personal discovery exercise. Allowing yourself to have a choice that serves you will absolutely feel scary at first.

Feel the fear and do it anyway.

You are allowed to have needs and wants. You are allowed to make space for those needs and wants. Give yourself permission to be a priority. Let go of the story that this is selfish. That is a story that doesn't serve you. Spend some time determining what makes you feel safe. When do you feel respected, and who are the people that make you feel this way?

As I mentioned, the biggest obstacle that you may feel when setting boundaries is fear!

➤ Fear of people not liking you.

➤ Fear of rejection.

➤ Fear of being unlovable.

➤ Fear of confrontation.

➤ Fear of abandonment.

➤ Fear of disappointing people.

But the truth is, those who love and support you unconditionally will not abandon you. Those who value you will respect your boundaries. It is natural when you try something new that there may be some pushback. Do not confuse or conflate this by thinking that certain people do not respect you. It may just upset the relationship dynamic initially, but a new pattern will emerge. Most good people do not want you to feel overwhelmed or devalued. Power dynamics get established and because of fear, both parties stay locked into the dynamic. You are allowed to disrupt the power dynamic of a relationship that doesn't respect your boundaries. Worthwhile relationships are able to grow and evolve over time.

Most good people do not want you to feel overwhelmed or devalued.

So, breathe deeply and give yourself immense compassion and empathy as you start this practice of personal discovery. You will get there. It will feel new and scary at first. You are building a new muscle, a new skill that asks you to choose what keeps you safe, not what is the most accommodating of others. The mindset shift begins and ends with you because you, dear heart, must become comfortable in your power. The power of determining who gets access to you and how they may access you. I know I am not alone in never having been taught healthy boundaries. Learn from me and this book and practice radical acceptance for learning this new skill. Start small by making commitments to yourself and following through on them.

> *"Your personal boundaries protect the inner core of your identity and your right to choices."*
> –Gerard Manley Hopkins, Poet & Jesuit Priest

Here's a small boundary you can set for yourself to practice. Set a bedtime and wake time and maintain this for three days. Fulfilling this commitment you've made to yourself will build up your self-trust. Reward yourself with something to mark this boundary of time. A walk in the park with a baked good, a new book, a dinner date, or a movie. Anything that lights you up. Celebrating new habits and skill-building creates new neural pathways that support change. You do something new and scary, then reward yourself, and your brain will recognize future changes as something positive. When you can create a new pattern that you can rely on within yourself it will bolster your confidence to set a boundary with a friend or family member. This is also a way to build the positive noticing circuitry. It really is that simple: notice when you do something positive and allow yourself to receive recognition from yourself.

You get to establish boundaries at every step of every relationship. If you are in a marriage or relationship, you can adjust your boundaries at any time along the way. If you are dating, having boundaries will help you determine who gets more access to you.

You teach people how to treat you.

This is a bold statement and one that can feel insincere if you have suffered from abuse. I understand this. If you have had your trust broken by someone, it can feel impossible to shift the dynamic. Fear from a past traumatic experience is real and one that needs baby steps to help you build your confidence. Start small by not answering the phone or limiting the time you talk to them when that person calls. Insulate yourself with friends and commitments to avoid spending time with them. It is very common to have someone in your immediate family system betray your boundaries. When you embark on this strategy, giving yourself small, actionable steps to achieve your boundary works best. You are allowed to take your energy back and learn how to create a sense of safety when you are dealing with unsafe people, places, and things.

There are people who will continue to trespass over your boundaries, even when you will lay out a clear plan on how to communicate with you. They will disregard it entirely. This is not on you; some people are difficult.

My client Chloe was working with a youth who was having difficulties. The youth did not want to continue her gymnastics, always having a reason why she couldn't make the class. The youth began texting Chloe to tell her when she would show up. The youth is only 11 years old. Chloe, not feeling comfortable dealing with a child around scheduling and administration (she would no sooner talk to the youth about billing than would allow the youth to dictate the terms of a set schedule), emailed the mother. She told the mother why keeping to the schedule was important for her daughter and asked that the mother call her privately or book an in-person session to discuss her daughter's training. The next day, the mother showed up at the gym with her daughter and barged into Chloe's office. The mother came out firing, reprimanding Chloe for not texting the daughter back, and then, within seconds, the father showed up. Chloe was taken aback and unsure how to manage the fact that this woman completely disregarded the boundaries and terms she had laid out in the email. Also, she was floored that she now had to manage the whole family on an impromptu logistics meeting that felt more like a counselling session.

The thing is, Chloe had issues with this client in the past. She had previously laid out terms that the mother challenged her on. For example, when to show up for class, how to support the youth at home, and when to submit payment. Even though Chloe was setting the terms on how she wanted to be treated, this client repeatedly disrespected those boundaries. This client is difficult and requires repetitive, consistent boundary setting. Chloe does an amazing job at keeping her dealings professional and understands that difficult people will cause conflict when they are uncomfortable with boundaries. Chloe knows that at any time, she can disengage with this family and stop teaching the girl, but she also knows that every time she has to adjust and repeat a standard, she is exercising her boundary muscle.

How to Handle Pushback on Your Boundaries

There are five common boundary pushback tactics that difficult people and predators portray. This is called a pushback because they are pushing back against the boundary, usually in a way that feels conversational or requires you to double down and be firm. A predator uses this tactic to challenge how resolute you are with your boundaries. A difficult person uses this when they themselves don't have healthy PEMS hygiene and do not know how to respect boundaries. The difficult people are not necessarily bad; they just require more effort. Sometimes, you will be game and up to it, and other times, you will avoid interactions with them because you don't have the energy.

Here are the five common boundary pushback tactics to be aware of that both difficult people and predators will employ:

1. **Questioning**: "What's your problem?" "Can't I ask you about your life?" "Why are you so sensitive?" "Who do you think you are?"

2. **Challenging:** "What are you going to do about it?" "You think you are so special?" "Why would that scare me?" "You think you can stop me?"

3. **Retaliation and Slander:** The difficult person or perpetrator will seek ways to damage your reputation or humiliate you. They may slander your name and say you are difficult to work with when they don't like your boundaries. A perpetrator knows no bounds when it comes to ways they will try to discredit you. They are all about outlandish gall and using manipulation to dominate someone. They will start rumours about you to diminish your achievements or reputation.

4. **Trivializing the Incident:** "Don't flatter yourself." "You must think you are really important." "As if I would do that." "You're not that special."

5. **Humiliation:** The difficult person may try shaming you in front of people to make you feel silly. They may mock you and conflate their history with you, saying things like, "Oh, so you think that we all just sit around waiting for you to bless us with your presence when we all know you never show up on time." The shame and blame game is to throw the focus off of them and make you feel small and terrible.

In addition to these five pushbacks, a good indicator that someone doesn't respect your boundaries is the talking trap: They keep talking and low-key resisting or challenging you to either reassert yourself or make them comfortable. This looks like them asking you to justify your opinion or position on an issue, trying to change your mind, or continually talking about the issue or subject after you have made your decision clear. It is a sad fact that many people employ low-key manipulation when communicating, especially when they themselves have never learned healthy boundaries. Well-intentioned people can be brought back on track because, for many of them, this manipulative communication style is unconscious. A predator is not well-intentioned. Their aim is to trap you into talking so as to confuse you, make you feel fatigued, and persuade you to do something you don't want to do. A predator's aim is to have you abandon your boundaries.

Now that you can recognize a pushback, you can anticipate it and respond accordingly. Moving forward, you get to teach people how you wish to be treated. You will feel scared, but do it anyway. What sounds like a simple thing, for example, to decline a lunch date with a group of friends that make you feel small, will feel HUGE because you are disrupting a pattern. A pattern that you learned from nice girl programming. The pattern of self-abandoning.

As discussed, self-abandoning is a conditioned response that people employ when they deem the effort needed to set a boundary or resolve a situation will be more of a hassle or will cause conflict, and so they do what is perceived to be easiest. In casual relationships with peers, clients, family, and friends, this pattern can whittle away self-esteem and confidence. Only in the face of someone who is violent or physically abusive does self-abandoning work as a self-defence strategy.

Looking back at our earlier example, Chloe was not self-abandoning because she was aware and diligent. She was using it as a strength-building exercise. She knows now that when she asserts herself, there will be people who will look for the sidestep or workaround, the people who directly and intentionally disrespect boundaries. If the pattern of self-abandonment shows up, meaning Chloe finds herself not saying what she needs, or if Chloe finds herself putting the mother's demands before her own, Chloe knows to cease teaching this youth.

Boundaries are not metaphorical walls that you need to erect to restrict people's access to you or your PEMS hygiene system. Boundaries are a safeguard; they help you create space for yourself. A physical boundary I use when I train in jiu-jitsu is deciding who gets to touch me. I choose who I train with, who I grapple with, or practice techniques with. If I feel a discordant energy with someone I have chosen, there is a mental, emotional, internal, rapid-fire checklist I analyse, and if it is conclusive, I stop training with them. I do not explain to them why I feel unsafe or give them an explanation for why I feel the way I do. It is not important to relay that. I simply excuse myself, inform my instructor if it is that type of class, or just bring someone new in.

A physical boundary can be established by using your voice and a hand gesture. In public, stop and ask someone approaching you, "Can I help you?" and put up your hand. This will interrupt their advance as you are using communication and body language to convey a boundary. You are allowed to ask someone to move further away from you, even if you were comfortable at first and then became uncomfortable. Someone who is family and hanging out on the couch with you or a stranger in a lineup. Simply ask, "Can you step over there?" or "Can you scooch over there?" You are allowed to communicate this and not explain why. You have permission to execute any physical, emotional, or mental boundary at any time.

Here are some helpful phrases for saying no:[24]

I can't give you an answer right now. Will you check back with me?

I want to, but I'm unable to.

I'm not able to commit to that right now.

I really appreciate you asking me, but I can't do it.

I understand you really need my help, but I'm just not able to say yes to that. I'm so sorry.

I'm going to say no for now. I'll let you know if something changes.

I'm honoured that you would ask me, but my answer is no.

No, I can't do that, but here's what I can do…

I just don't have that to give right now.

---

[24] Courtesy of Julie de Azevedo Hanks, PhD, MSW, LCSW

Remember:

Boundaries define where you end and someone else begins!

It may feel unsafe to set boundaries if you have never been taught to have boundaries. This unsafe feeling can be transmuted into safety and power, building up your confidence and self-trust.

It is okay to feel awkward at first when learning a new skill. Healthy boundaries are challenging when you first begin.

It can take several attempts to set healthy boundaries until you build a new circuitry that feels comfortable.

You are allowed to feel unsure or scared and still have boundaries.

You do not have to have perfect execution.

You can change your mind at any time with anyone.

You got this!

I believe in you!

CHAPTER 13

Situational Awareness

Situational awareness is having knowledge of your surroundings. This includes the people, places, and things that you encounter in everyday life. Situational awareness is having a plan; being prepared is being aware! I want you to know how to move around the world with a safety state of mind, which means honing your ability to perceive the environment that you put yourself in. As you learn how to trust your gut instincts, your ability to survive, escape, and control negative situations and potential threats will improve. Moving forward, I want you to ask yourself: "What is the safest thing for me to do?" This phrase will ensure you formulate a plan to anticipate future outings, re-assess current situations, and propel your actions that provide safety.

What to Look for When You Are Out and About:

▸▸ Locate the exits and entrances in any closed space, restaurant, or event you go to. If you need to leave and the main entrance is blocked, having already sussed out alternative routes upon arriving will help you remain calm and confident so you can remove yourself from the location of danger or threat.

▸ Identify where support personnel, staff, or facilitators are located. Knowing ahead of time who can assist you in the event that you need help is the safest strategy.

> At the lake, where are the lifeguards or the first aid unit? In the event that you need support or help, do you know where to go?

> At a concert, where are the security staff positioned? Did you identify the exits?

> In a public space, where are the support staff or the event facilitators? Did you identify the exits, and do you know the safest, quickest way to leave this event?

> At a party, whose house are you at? What is the address? Should you need to call a ride or have someone come and get you, do you know where you are?

> At school, where is the security personnel and information office? Do you know the names of the support staff that mind your children?

> At a club or bar, where is security? Identify the exits from the bar and the bar location at the onset. How easy is it to get into? How easy is it to leave the location?

▸ When you get into an elevator, stand near the button panel should you need to call for help. Get off the elevator even if you are not on your floor or if you feel uncomfortable with someone who is riding with you. Go into an office or knock on a door and get assistance if you are scared or feel like you are being followed. Avoid going directly to your room with your head down and not looking behind you before and after you open the door.

▸ In a parking garage, do not park near columns or dark, secluded areas like stairwells or stone pillars. If this means walking extra so you can have a clear line of sight of your vehicle, do it. Know if this garage has security personnel or a booth that you can go to for assistance. Know where the elevators are and how to exit the garage safely.

▶▶ When parking your vehicle in other circumstances, avoid alleyways or recessed doorways. Have knowledge of the surrounding area if you are new to that location. Download a map of facilities or parks that list the location of personnel ahead of time. Plan your route, your parking, and your walk route to the building or meeting place.

When Travelling, Familiarize Yourself With:

▶▶ Which areas of the town or region that you are visiting have heavy drug use or parks that are frequented by addicts or drug dealers. Know which areas in the town you are visiting have a high incidence of crime.

▶▶ Check with the concierge about neighbourhoods to avoid. They may not be obvious or come up on the usual internet searches. Ethnicity and cultural sensitivities can influence behaviour patterns.

▶▶ Leave notice with the front desk as to your outings, especially if you are travelling alone. Tell the staff if you are going on a hike or a group tour, etc.

▶▶ Arrange your travel for the first night, including how to get from the airport or train station, and book a hotel. Choose a hotel that is in a GOOD location. Even if you want to do a walkabout or an Eat, Pray, Love vibe and wing it, having a safe arrival point/location is the safest bet. You can improvise from there by following these guidelines, but you need an anchor for your arrival that can function as a launch pad.

▶▶ Give your itinerary to friends or family, with the anchor points for where you will be and when.

▸▸ Try to arrive at new locations during the day as opposed to night-time. Schedule flights and transportation to accommodate daytime arrivals as much as possible. It is so much easier to get your bearings in the light of day!

▸▸ Never tell anyone that you are travelling alone or where you are staying. Use the do not disturb sign for your door and leave the TV on and a light. If you can, ask for a second set of slippers from the hotel to leave by the door, indicating that there are two people staying in a room. If you are camping, always put out two towels on the clothesline, set up two chairs by the fire pit, and bring extra shoes to give the impression of more than one person.

▸▸ Carry a paper map or maps that work offline on your phone and carry a card for the hotel/location you are staying at for ease of reference in case someone needs to assist you. Have your pertinent documents stored safely on your person as well when you are out and about. Copy of passport, driver's license, travel insurance, emergency contact, etc.

▸▸ Avoid overconsumption of alcohol to keep a clear head.

▸▸ Try to travel light and keep your belongings with you in the back seat as opposed to the trunk. Having all your belongings makes it easier if you need to get out of the car and move your location from where you are.

Avoidance is a key personal protection and self-defence technique, so avoid being in places where you are likely to enter into a confrontation or be attacked. Avoid going to bars or contentious sporting events at night. Even during the day, if there is a group of rowdy guests or if you feel uncomfortable at any time, leave. I know that sounds simple, but by practicing situational awareness, you are planning your safety in the world as you move about. Don't worry if this hasn't been on your radar and you are just learning now because once you start, having a safety state of mind will become second nature.

Situational awareness also includes being aware of what is near you or on you that could be used as a potential self-defence tool. What objects on your person could be utilized should bodily harm or an attack occur?

- **Dog leash**: Can be used to whip or choke someone.

- **Umbrella**: Can be used to create distance, a boundary, or a perimeter. It can also be used to hit or jab a potential attacker.

- **Key chain**: You can have an implement on your keychain, such as a flashlight, a whistle or a kubotan. A kubotan is a simple rod, with no blades or sharp edges, made out of metal or high strength plastic. It was developed by a martial artist and law enforcement trainer, named Takayuki Kubota in the 1960's.

- **Rock or stick**: Can be used whilst hiking, running, or walking to create a distraction or distance between you and a potential threat.

- **Chair**: Can be used to create a boundary, to block a door, or as a shield.

- **Tray or book**: Can be used to hit a threat or as a shield.

- **Lid on the toilet tank**: Can be used as a shield or a weapon.

- **Belt**: Can be used to create distance between you and a threat by striking or whipping or to tie up limbs.

- **Purse or bag**: Can be used as a shield or a striking weapon. You can also throw it at someone.

- **Water bottle**: Can be used to strike someone.

I understand that it can be unnerving to think about having to use an object in your vicinity or on your person in a self-defence scenario, so take a deep breath. Bringing awareness to the opportunities at hand

and having a plan will expand your consciousness into thinking about personal protection.

Practicing personal protection strategies primes you to:

- ▶▶ acclimatize your nerves to a potentiality.

- ▶▶ bolster your confidence.

- ▶▶ learn how to problem-solve.

- ▶▶ practice situational awareness, all the time.

If you are dating or going somewhere with a new person or group of people, here are some things to prepare and keep in mind while you're out:

- ▶▶ Establish a code phrase with your closest friends, parents, or significant other. This allows you to communicate that you need an out when you call them or text them. Arranging this ahead of time is planning for success. Something as simple as "Aunt Violet is coming over" or a code word, like "pistachio," will work. Having a plan in place to use a code phrase will eliminate any awkwardness you may feel trying to establish an exit strategy or ride home once you get a gut instinct that you need to leave. It gives you an "out" that you can claim is beyond your control and doesn't require you to articulate your feelings. It is an excellent exit strategy that removes any liability from you. Saying the code word notifies those in your circle of trust that you need help without letting anyone else know.

- ▶▶ Avoid getting a ride in the car with people you do not know well. Do not share an Uber or cab with your date at the end of the night. Have a strategy in place for arriving and leaving that keeps you safe.

▸▸ Wherever the date is taking place, familiarize yourself with the exits and support staff. Opt for a seat that keeps your line of sight in view of the door. That way, you can clock who is joining the space you are in. Being able to see your way out can also provide a sense of comfort in any situation.

▸▸ Avoid having a date in your house or apartment until much, much later in the relationship.

The chapter on predatory behaviour in this book has more details about what to be aware of when dating and offers more tips on how to build personal protection strategies when meeting new people.

For the Kids and Youths in Your Life:

▸▸ Teach them situational awareness and to have a plan.

▸▸ Give them a code phrase they can use when they are out in the world that signals they need you to pick them up. Always let them know they have a safe way to get home.

▸▸ When they go to a party or event, ask them:

➤ Will parents be there, and if not, who will be supervising?

➤ Will there be alcohol or drugs involved?

➤ How will they be getting there and leaving?

➤ If they have a ride, who is it with?

➤ What if the people they are with decide to drink?

➤ What is their plan A and their plan B?

▸▸ Teach and model to them how to trust their gut! Make sure they know they can leave any situation if they get uncomfortable at any time.

▸▸ Tell them not to get isolated from their friends.

▶▶ Tell them to avoid watching inappropriate behaviour i.e., a girl who is forced to keg it or a boy who is bullied into doing a stunt. Seeing someone being manipulated into a behaviour that is risky elevates a crowd's energy and leaves a large margin for things to go wrong! This is tricky with youths, but having a conversation is the first step. Modelling behaviour that encourages self-esteem, autonomy, and knowing right from wrong will equip them with strong personal protection options. Teaching them not to go along with the group mentality of the weirdly inappropriate humiliation rituals of youth (keg, stunts, pranks) is an often overlooked conversation, but one that is important!

When my kids were little, we would go to the mall, and I would tell them to go ask a security guard or an attendant for directions. I did this to condition them to feel confident asking for help in public situations and train them to use their voice in public with persons of authority. This process helps to demystify what reaching out for help and support can look like. I would also trust their feedback should they choose someone else or decline my nomination.

Teaching kids that their gut instincts are valuable is a tremendous tool for blocking gut punches in the future.

CHAPTER **14**

Threat Cues

A threat cue is an indicator of harm, a suggestion of menace, or a warning that something or someone is about to pop off or do something threatening. Threat cues can be non-verbal shifts in body language, like the colour of someone's face changing, or a vocalized threat, like someone cursing or yelling at you.

Body Language Threat Cues

✧ Face turns red or colour drains

✧ Eyes narrow, glaze over, or become expressionless

✧ Veins start to show on the forehead or in the neck

✧ Fists are clenched

✧ Lips tighten up

✧ Voice starts to get scratchy or becomes monotone

✧ Trouble speaking well or speaking rapidly (something out of the norm or regular for the person)

✧ Clearing of the throat

✧ Breathing changes (this can be an indicator of adrenaline)

✧ Sweating

✧ They enter attack mode

Behavioural Threat Cues

⋈ Resisting your request and or commands

⋈ Obviously ignoring you (this could be a primer for a sneak attack)

⋈ Asking you a lot of questions or throwing your questions back at you

⋈ Not making eye contact or looking right through you

⋈ Exhibiting excessively exaggerated movements

⋈ Trying to distract you

⋈ Not acting in a normal fashion

⋈ Pacing, turning, pointing, threatening with fists, arms bent and entangled, hands on hips

⋈ Not moving or staring blankly (something out of the norm or regular for the person)

    ⋈ Invading your personal space

    ⋈ Crowding

    ⋈ Stepping right up in your face (may happen with people who have been drinking at a club or party that can not hear you in a venue with loud music, so be sure to watch for other cues)

    ⋈ Rushing right up to you

So, now that we've covered some of the different threat cues you need to look out for, what does attack mode look like? This is when someone assumes a 'fight stance' or a 'bladed stance,' often right before they attack or strike out.

Here are some signs that someone is entering attack mode:

- ►► Lowering their centre of gravity
- ►► Head back, shoulder back, i.e. karate style
- ►► Shoulders hunched and chin tucked, i.e. boxing style
- ►► Crouch with more weight on the front foot, i.e. grappling style
- ►► Rocking or shifting back and forth
- ►► Bouncing on one's toes to find a rhythm
- ►► Shaking their hands and fingers to get the blood or feeling in them (this is caused when adrenaline floods the body)
- ►► Staring at a target on your body, like the neck, knees, or midsection, before getting ready to hit it.
- ►► Eye movement towards a potential weapon, i.e. a bottle, chair, pool cue, garden shears, rake, shovel, glassware, stick, etc.

Unseen weapons may be present. Here are some cues you can look for to tell if this is the case:

- ►► When a person presents themselves, one or both of their hands are hidden.
- ►► When a person moves their hands to be hidden from view.
- ►► When a person has their hands in a palming position or a closed position.
- ►► When a person moves their hand towards their pockets, bag, fanny sack, purse, inside of coat, behind their back, etc. A change of movement where the hands could be reaching for something is a cue.
- ►► They have a duffel bag in the back seat of the car or with them on an outing that is not camping or just coming from the gym/dojo.

Familiarizing yourself with threat cues will hone your awareness. Having these logged in a mental file will alert you if you are presented with a situation. You need to know how to recognize non-verbal gestures so you can be safe around people, places, and things. Knowing what to be mindful of and how to be aware is part of your situational awareness.

Adding the ability to recognize a threat cue to your PEMS toolkit will allow you to make decisions, problem-solve, avoid, and escape a possible attack or confrontation.

CHAPTER 15

Predatory Behaviour

When I speak about predatory behaviour, I am profiling someone who stalks, recruits, and/or attacks another with a systemized attitude. The mindset of a predator is calculated.

A predator is also usually not a random stranger lurking in the bushes but, more likely, is an acquaintance, a friend, or a family member. According to an article by Lucy Adams, a BBC Correspondent, more than 90% of rape and sexual assault victims know their attacker. 90%! Researchers from Glasgow University said it was a popular misconception that most attackers were strangers. The study looked at the 991 women in Scotland who went through an advocacy programme, which ran for 18 months. It found that despite many reforms to rape laws, women still suffered as a result of delays and the impersonal nature of the justice system.

The study[25] also found:

- ▶▶ Just 9% of perpetrators were strangers to the victim
- ▶▶ 23% of women were assaulted by a partner or ex-partner

---

[25]Violent deaths of women in Canada increased in 2020, study finds. CBC News. https://www.cbc.ca/news/canada/femicide-canada-1.5953953

▶▶ 24% were assaulted by a family member

▶▶ 44% were assaulted by "another known person"

▶▶ 32% were reported to the police more than two years after the incident

▶▶ More than 20% of the women took more than 10 years to report their ordeal to the police

▶▶ 22% had not reported their assaults to the police at all.

Though the study cited above is on women, men are 67% more likely to be attacked or assaulted by someone known to them as well. Overwhelmingly, research[26] shows that the majority of people who perpetrate sexual assault against men are other men, though women can and do commit sexual violence. Assault and danger is rarely a boogeyman lurking in the bushes. The fact that you are most likely to be assaulted by someone known to you makes it paramount for you to understand what your default survival state is and practice PEMS hygiene.

In order for you to pick up on social cues and read someone's intentions, you need to know where you begin and end, so to speak. You need to have a practice that brings you into your body so you can move safely and with confidence. Understanding your nervous system blueprint and how trauma affects your intuition will give you insight into who and what you respond to and why instinctually. This is important information. Avoiding potentially dangerous situations, using your awareness to determine who should have access to you, and cultivating an empowered attitude are the strategies you need to develop. Your life changes when you learn the survive and thrive mindset because you will feel emboldened to claim your space!

---

[26] Choudhary, E., Gunzler, D., Tu, X., & Bossarte, R. (2012). *Epidemiological Characteristics of Male Sexual Assault in a Criminological Database.* Journal of Interpersonal Violence, 27(3), 523-546.

By now, you can understand when your boundaries have gotten violated and how re-organizing your nervous system supports your safety, both energetically and physically. I want to be clear that there are, most definitely, situations in which someone wants to do you harm, and the only safe thing to do will be to act as compliant and agreeable as possible until you can safely create distance from them. There are violent people who need to dominate, overwhelm, and overpower with their speech and their behaviour. Let's dig into who those people are.

These people have ill intent. They have predatory behaviour whose aim is to prey upon you, using manipulation tactics disguised as harmless innuendos that are calculated and relentless. Please do not conflate an interpersonal relationship you have with a friend, family member, or co-worker who has poor social skills or awkward behaviour. Please make a mental note that there is a significant difference between someone who is socially awkward and has a pure heart and someone who is deviously calculating ways to overpower/intimidate/force you into a potentially very dangerous situation.

Predatory behaviour by someone you know can be a series of innocuous encounters whereby they are testing your boundaries. They are seeing how close they can get to you and whether or not you will stand up for yourself. This is a form of grooming/preparing a potential victim. This subtle grooming can be difficult to detect, and there are multiple ways they will test you. It should be noted that these encounters are compounding; they are not singular acts but rather a series of events where they are testing you/grooming you. To see how far they can go without protest and or consent from you. When you look back at the succession of inappropriate or uncomfortable interactions with said person, you can often clearly see how they were trying to manipulate you all along.

If you are a parent with children, you will want to take note of any adults who start to take an interest in your child. This can be someone from church, at their school, or in your family. Beware of them taking a special interest in your child or volunteering to babysit or be alone with them. You need to have discernment regarding who gets access to your child or teen. This is an important personal-defence strategy that you must employ as a parent. Being aware of the strategies a predator uses will aid in this discernment. Both boys and girls/men and women can be victims of predatory grooming! Someone with a predator mindset will violate trust and boundaries before they violate the law. They use charm and excessive flattery to win over the opposition.

Dr. Wendy Patrick, PHD,[27] a motivational speaker who trains worldwide on sexual assault detection and prevention, defines Grooming as "... *desensitizing a victim to inappropriate social or sexual advances through progressive boundary-probing, while at the same time developing a foundation of trust. It is a recipe for a power imbalance. The primary purpose of grooming is to normalize inappropriate behaviour. Whether pursuing sex, money, power, or just the thrill of inflicting emotional harm, predators use victims to benefit themselves.*"

Our collectively conditioned behaviours to be nice, put others first, and think well of others can hoodwink us into being deceived by someone's malicious intentions. Be safe over and above being polite! It is far better to be wrong and hurt someone's feelings than to be wrong and get HURT!! Men or women in positions of power who use that power to take advantage of someone systematically and for their own pleasure are harmful and predatory.

Take, for example, the story of Emma Healey,[28] a Canadian writer and poet from Toronto, Ontario. In her article, titled *Stories Like Passwords*,

---

[27] From an article published May 1, 2018, by Dr. Wendy L. Partick, J.D., Ph.D., titled, *The Stealthiest Predator*, in Psychology Today magazine.

[28] Her book, *Best Young Woman Job Book: A Memoir*, was published by Random House Canada in 2022. It was named best book of the year by both the Globe and Mail and Wired Magazine, shortlisted for the Trillium Book Award, and longlisted for the Leacock Medal. https://medium.com/the-hairpin/stories-like-passwords-bf04e46c3fb6

Emma describes how a 34-year-old teacher seduced her over the course of two years when she herself was 19.

He was a prominent professor who expressed interest in working on a project or two with Emma after reading some of her poems. They exchanged a few emails over the summer. She found out he was teaching a class the next semester and wanted to join, but the class was full. The professor said he would see what he could do.

The night before school started, he messaged her a casual invitation to meet for drinks.

Emma met him and his friends for drinks. He told her he didn't want to get her drunk as he ordered her another beer and a shot.

She describes the night as best she can remember in the article: closing out a bar, going to another bar upstairs, his friends disappearing, being back at her apartment, and watching him get dressed to leave.

Emma recounts how she felt *"gullible and stubborn and self-sure and shaky and guilty all at once."*[29] Their relationship encounters lasted two years, with the last interaction exhibiting the same incongruence of words and actions, dominating energy, and gross violation of boundaries as the first meetup.

A respected, feted professor tells a young woman he likes her work. He shows interest in her poetry and alludes to working together. As a new, aspiring artist this kind of attention would be dazzling. Emma wants to be in his class, and after some back-and-forth emails, an invitation to a bar to meet the professor and his colleagues seems like an opportunity.

Telling her he doesn't want to get her drunk but asking her to meet him in a bar and buying her multiple drinks is incoherent and inappropriate behaviour.

---

[29] Cited directly from the article titled *Stories Like Passwords* by Emma Healy in The Hairpin, October 11, 2014

He was 34, she was 19.

Emma illuminates how common this predatory behaviour is in the literary community she resides within. When she began to share her experience with other women, other women poured out similar stories. Thus, the title of her essay: *Stories Like Passwords*. Once initiated, the floodgates open, and women share, needing to be witnessed, needing to be validated, and needing to be reassured that it is not just them.

It is a devastating reality that in the self-defence and personal protection arena, society puts the onus on women to call out abuse. Society protects the abuser until it becomes obvious or difficult to ignore, which needs to change. As Emma poignantly writes in her article.

These issues are not simple ones to discuss or to deal with, and they do not develop—or change—overnight. There is a complex and tangled system of habits, behaviours, and assumptions in our communities that runs underneath our tendency to turn a blind eye to potentially predatory behaviour until it reaches a boiling point. These things are ingrained, and it's difficult to know how we might even begin to change them.

Typically, identifying predator behaviour occurs in reverse. It is only when looking at the compounding incidents over time that you recognize the traits of predatory behaviour. The main traits of predatory behaviour are a series of seemingly innocent or casual violations of trust, perpetual gaslighting, trespassing boundaries, and making you uncomfortable, bit by bit.

Predators go undetected using charm, wit, advantage, prestige, opportunity, and access. They usually remain unlabelled as such because it's not until women share stories with one another that they find out that they are dealing with the same person who has repeated predatory behaviour, and so they are the most dangerous.

Examples of predatory grooming include:

» Seeing how close they can get to you, standing closer than necessary, coming up behind you, and seeing how long it takes for you to recognize them.

» Touching you briefly in a pseudo-inappropriate way, like brushing past your breasts or thigh or having a lingering touch such as a hug that slides down your back to your hip or buttocks.

» Saying inappropriate things to you such as remarks on your physique. For example, saying something like

➤ "Are those rose buds on your chest?"

➤ "Those hips of yours are so inviting."

➤ "Dance for me."

➤ "You shouldn't wear that skirt if you didn't want my attention."

» Making sexual innuendos or crass jokes.

» Challenging your relationship status in a condescending or joking manner.

» Ingratiating themselves with your parents, your friends, your co-workers.

» Trying to isolate you from others by getting you alone in the hallway or away from a workplace, class, activity, or party.

» Showing up at your workplace or at any event you are at when they have little cause or justification for being there.

» Calling or messaging you without you having given them permission or access.

» Giving lavish gifts at the start of a relationship.

So, what can you do?

You cannot have a safe relationship with a predator.

Learn to recognize this behaviour so you can avoid future problems. Have clear boundaries. Find out where the metaphorical line in the sand is and leave when that line gets crossed. Do not let yourself be led into the talking trap, self gaslight and ignore the red flags and gut instincts. Be firm and non-compliant with the predator's behaviour. Like I said before, predators usually start by testing the waters and challenging you to see what they can get away with. They want to test you, repeatedly, to let your guard down. It may sound like a small thing, but practicing the personal protection strategies laid out in this book can eliminate the predator from seeing you as a victim! Thus avoiding much bigger, scarier problems down the road. This is not a victim-shaming statement at all. It is speaking to the fact that a predator is, in essence, a coward who preys on someone whom they perceive as weak, malleable and easily influenced. Knowing how they operate and what to look out for puts you ahead of their tactics. You cannot have a safe relationship with a predator. When you have an emotionally safe relationship with yourself, it is much easier to spot the signs of an unsafe relationship with others.

Bookmark the statements below.[30] Put them on your phone and practice saying them until you feel bold enough to embody them. Repeating these statements helps you develop emotional safety with yourself because they may be the first time you give yourself permission to feel them.

▸▸ My feelings matter

▸▸ I'm not overreacting/too sensitive/dramatic

▸▸ Having needs doesn't make me needy

---

[30] Cited from Divya Robin, Licensed Mental Health Counsellor (LMHC) Instagram @mindmatterswithdiv https://www.divyarobin.com/about

➤➤ I'm doing the best with what I have right now

➤➤ I'm enough, just as I am right now

➤➤ I'm allowed to take up space

➤➤ I am deserving of support or help

> I can take accountability for my actions (and how they impact others) while being gentle to myself

> I don't need to solve problems right now; I can give myself space to feel

> It's okay that this doesn't make sense right now

> I can slow down and take a deep breath

> I am safe

> I am allowed to rest

Recreating safety within happens when you can dismantle self-limiting beliefs and rewire your nervous system so you can accurately perceive when someone is welcoming or if someone is a threat.

Be aware of seemingly innocuous physical touching! The kind of touching that you are not sure is intentional but is inappropriate nonetheless. Why? Besides the obvious fact that you and only you decide who touches you, where they touch you, and when they touch you, this is the play of someone who is seeing what they can get away with. That is the behaviour of a potential predator. For example, you are at an outdoor concert with a group of friends. A guy you know stands too close to you and brushes his hands across your ass. You think this may be a mistake, but then he brushes across your breasts. Now you know it was intentional, inappropriate touching and that he is bold and unpredictable. If he is doing this in a group setting in front of others, who knows what else he is capable of? This guy has shown that he is unpredictable and potentially dangerous. Pointing your finger at him and calling him out in front of others is an option, but is that the safest thing to do?

The safest thing to do is to go stand by your girlfriend. Remove yourself from his immediate space. Tell her what he tried to do. Create an ally and enlist her to be the buffer. Meaning you stay by her and not by him. If he tries to regain his position, tell him you are more comfortable standing beside your girlfriend. You can ask your girlfriend to go to the bathroom with you to shift the dynamic. Do not worry about hurting his feelings because taking care of yourself is more important, and you need to trust the vibe you are getting from this guy.

Here are some scenarios of predatory behaviour:

Scenario 1

You are at work and the really cute guy that all the women have a low-key crush on starts showing up in the lunchroom when you are there alone. He stands too close and remarks that he really likes your shirt. The next time, he stands too close and tells you likes your shoes. The next time, he makes a sexual innuendo about his lunch. He always stands too close to you, for longer than you're comfortable. He always manages to block your exit. He is boxing you in and testing you. First with flattery and then with sexual innuendo and with his domineering body language.

What do you do?

You like this guy, or rather, you like the way he looks. You like the fact that he is popular. You feel special that he is paying attention to you but also uncomfortable with him being in your space.

This is an opportunity for you to practice boundaries.

Option 1: You get flustered, mumble something, look down, slightly turn your back towards him, and wait for him to leave. (*Never turn your back on someone who violates your boundaries, as scary as that can be. I KNOW just taking up space can feel scary and intimidating!)

Option 2: You turn and face him and say, "Thanks. Can you back up please? You're a bit close." You make eye contact, and your voice is calm, steady, and clear. Your hands come up as you use your words and you create a physical boundary.

Your behaviour in option one leaves you unprotected. It allows him to have dominance, rewarding his desire to make you uncomfortable. This will register as a success to a potential predator; they are always looking for subtle ways to gain an advantage so they can take advantage.

With option two, you have stated a boundary, you use an assertive, friendly communication style, and you potentially create a witness should someone see you in the lunchroom. Your body language will be read and interpreted as you saying no thank you. You haven't said or done anything provoking; you simply claimed your space and made sure to communicate what you were needing in that moment.

Scenario 2

You go on a coffee date with a girl that you've been messaging with for a while. She is super engaged with listening and eager with her questions. She asks about your schedule, your friends, and your routine. She alludes to a past relationship, saying her ex was a nightmare. You leave it open for a second date and offer to call her later.

At work the next day, when you go for lunch, she is at your lunch place. She had called the previous night, and you already have a date set up for later in the week. You say hi and ask what she is doing there. She replies, saying she just needed to see you. Later that night, you get multiple texts, and the next morning, she sends your favourite book,

The RomCom era has done us all a great disservice by highlighting persistence as swoon-worthy.

that you mentioned on your first date, to your work. You get a notification that she has friended a collection of your friends on social media. She is at your workplace when you finish for the day and asks you if you have time for a quick bite to eat.

Does this sound romantic? Does she seem like she is just a super charmer and simply cannot get enough of you? The RomCom era has done us all a great disservice by highlighting persistence as swoon-worthy when it is usually cleverly cloaked predatory behaviour. Too much, too soon.

What do you do?

Option 1: You feel so special. This gal must really like you, so you agree to all of it and count yourself lucky.

Option 2: You tell her there is something you need to finish at work that you just remembered, and you go back to find a colleague or friend who can accompany you home. If there isn't anyone, you stay at work and call a friend to meet you. You text the new gal and say you cannot have dinner tonight. You cancel the upcoming dinner date. You let her know that you need to move much slower. For example, friending your friends before you have had a chance to get to know each other isn't cool. If she respects what you ask for, there may be an opportunity to pursue this, but if she blames you for leading her on or pressures you into seeing her, RED FLAG!

Here are some red flags to be mindful of when meeting someone new:

▸▸ Expressing jealousy

▸▸ Speaking ill of past relationships/women

- Challenging physical boundaries

- Pushing sexual advancement and activities

- Using manipulative speech and actions

- Creating dependency (wanting to pick you up, drive you, chaperone you, etc.)

So often, we dismiss our gut reactions to a person, place, or thing because we want to be polite. How many times have you said to yourself, "I don't want to overreact or be dramatic."

We are conditioned to gaslight ourselves! We second-guess ourselves, wondering if we are too sensitive or if they really meant to make us uncomfortable, etc. We are taught to self-minimize and not make a big deal out of 'it.' Collectively, we are taught to protect the abuser. The clever cloaks for deniability of experience that make us question if that really happened? Did I imagine it? Here's the thing though, you know when someone crosses a line because it feels icky. You know when someone tries to take advantage of your kindness, it feels different. Subtle abuse tactics and grooming feel gross, too. I want the examples here to be your rear-view mirror so you can identify it more readily in your life.

We are conditioned to gaslight ourselves!

I am not ignorant of the major power imbalance that exists in our society, where male privilege and dominance are the pervasive themes that women must navigate within. Society needs to change. Culturally, we need to learn how to protect our girls and women better. Men need to speak up and stand up for the girls and women. More emphasis should be put on teaching boys not to hurt girls, instead of putting the responsibility on girls to protect themselves. The sad truth is that there are bad people who do bad things. Violence against women is one of those very bad things. Arming yourself with this knowledge does not excuse the fact that this should change. Knowing how predators operate helps you. They are always looking for an advantage or a way in, and they use excessive flattery to get it. Don't be charmed. A predator will seek to overpower you and gain any advantage they can, whether that be financially, sexually, emotionally, or professionally. Knowing how to avoid and create distance between you and them is the best strategy for the moment.

CHAPTER **16**

Somatic Experiencing 101

"Taking time is very important—as body time is much
slower than cognitive time or emotional time."
–Dr. Peter Levine

Somatic experiencing (SE) is a body-based approach to healing trauma developed by Peter Levine, PhD, that is specifically focussed on drawing our attention back to the body. This practice focuses on supporting the optimal functioning of your nervous system and using the body to feel itself. Somatic experiencing is not interested in revisiting the episodes or events that have caused interpersonal difficulties or caused big T or little t trauma. The focus in SE is to bring you into your body so you can learn how to feel again. SE is especially poignant if you have a pattern of hyperarousal or hypoarousal behaviours such as; panic, anxiety, depression, or shutdown tendencies. SE is incredibly beneficial in helping you mitigate the inevitable and overwhelming accompanying PEMS body crash that is so prevalent in this demanding, modern world.

SE accompanies yoga therapy and jiu-jitsu specifically because it teaches you how to regulate the large number of inputs and requests and the amount of body exploration required in these disciplines. The body keeps a record of everything that happens to you. When you do movement practice, there will be an influx of inevitable sensations, feelings, and emotions that arise, re-surface, and make themselves known to you. For some, this experience will be pleasant. There will be a leveling up of ability and low disruption in the nervous system.

Somatic experiencing gives you a new language to reorganize the feelings that you feel.

However, for many, the nervous system will become activated due to past inputs, stored survival responses, and the habituated disorganization of their defence system due to chronic neglect and mismanagement. Somatic experiencing gives you a new language to reorganize the feelings that you feel. It gives you exploratory tools to expand your understanding of how to manage your body when it is triggered, activated, numb, or tuned out. SE focuses our primary attention on body sensations, urges, emotions, motions, and imagery. It also prioritizes bottom-up processing over top-down processing, meaning feeling with the body first as opposed to intellectualizing from the mind.

Before we get into the SE techniques, we need to cover the idea of containment. Containment is similar to your window of tolerance from the Gut Punch chapter. Remember, your window of tolerance is the optimal emotional "zone" you can exist in, to best function and thrive in everyday life. Think of containment as the overall vessel of your PEMS hygiene system. You know when you have reached your limit, emotionally, mentally, or physically. For example, you have dug out the old hedge in the backyard, and your back, knees, and muscles let you know that you are done. Or you just did your year-end taxes, planned the kids' graduation celebration, paid the bills for the month, and ordered all the supplies for the celebration. You are done. This is understanding your containment. In the chapters on awareness, avoidance, and situational awareness, you became reacquainted with how to check in with yourself. Learning how to determine when your energy is available to produce an output and when you need input is something you'll need to explore continually. Containment refers to that which you are able to hold at a specific time. When I had the flu, I did not feel like my containment potential could accommodate leaving the house and getting chores done. Containment is your ability to hold space within your body-mind for potential adverse events and big emotions. As I have continued along my martial arts career, I have developed a resiliency that supports my containment. Before I understood the language of nervous system regulation, my window of tolerance for new experiences and new levels of training was modest and sometimes erratic. Having C-PTSD means the optimal zone for living well, is a very fluid, active, movable goal post. Before I understood this new language and crafted the PEMS hygiene model, I experienced setbacks as a forever thing and misjudged how much I was healing. By learning these SE techniques and feeling witnessed my window of tolerance has expanded I can now anticipate and handle future events that will inevitably occur with a safer, more regulated container. What used to push me over the edge with anxiety and rumination, now rolls off my back as an expected ebb and flow of contraction and expansion.

Now, let's look at three somatic experiencing techniques that are interchangeable as self-defence strategies and nervous system regulation techniques. These techniques will help you heal your trauma from the inside out so you can listen to your gut instincts more accurately. You can use SE techniques on the mat when you are doing yoga or jiu-jitsu, on the golf course, or at the gym. You can even use them when you are visiting family! Learning these three SE techniques is going to help you safely anchor into how you are feeling and consciously tone your nervous system. As with all the other personal protection strategies I am teaching you, go slowly with these. Allow them to percolate in your mind. Play with them and add them to your PEMS hygiene tool kit.

Grounding & Orientation

Grounding and Orientation functions as the antidote to disconnection. Learning how to orient yourself to your surroundings pulls your focus into the present state. I should mention that there is a practice called grounding that involves getting your feet on the earth with no shoes. Though this is a valuable tool, and one I highly recommend, this is not the grounding I am referring to here. Grounding means to secure or pull your focus into the present moment. Orientation is to see, hear, and feel what is around you in your physical environment to anchor your consciousness. Grounding and orientation are interchangeable words for this technique. Why would you need to use grounding and orientation? If you are starting to panic or dissociate due to triggering inputs, being able to anchor your mind into the exact space you are in by orienting yourself—naming what you can see, feel, hear, and touch—can disrupt this pattern or nervous system response. Grounding and orientation can prevent you from going into a full panic, shutdown, or dissociative state.

You can use grounding and orientation when you feel the emotional toll of people, places, and things. Perhaps you have that one friend who forgets to ask permission before brain-dumping chaotic stories onto your lap. You feel your overwhelm peak when she un-solicitously brain dumps because you do not have the containment for any more drama or chaos. Ground yourself and orientate to your surroundings when that overwhelm kicks in. Look around yourself and name what you can see. Count out at least four items. Then, name what you hear and feel the clothes touching your body. This will anchor your mind consciously to your surroundings, grounding and orienting you to your physical, now moment.

One of my students, Ramani, has C-PTSD and has a tendency to vacate both mentally and emotionally. When she panics or is overwhelmed with processing information, it sets off her dissociative button. This sometimes happens when she is busy practicing jiu-jitsu. When she is on the mat and about to dissociate, she uses grounding and orienting to stay present in the moment. She feels the texture of the lapel on her gi and runs her hand along the tatami (the Japanese mat surface). Ramani will name what she can see in her mind and call out the items in her mind's eye, counting at least four so she can orient herself in the room. She quietly notes what she can hear in the room: other students, the fan, the traffic, and the birds outside the open window. She mouths the names of the other students.

Now, this is a room she has been in for over ten years. This familiarity is helpful, but without the presence of mind to call her focus into the room by naming what she can see, hear, and feel, being in a familiar space doesn't mean as much as we might think. She uses these grounding and orientating strategies to keep her present and to override the pattern, the past pain points, and the stored survival response that shows up when she becomes hyper-aroused or hypo-aroused.

Grounding and orientation can even be helpful in largely pleasant situations. Say you had a lovely evening out on a first date. You shared dinner in a nice restaurant, and now your date is offering to drive you home. You have all these new inputs of a pleasant shared experience, but you are only just getting to know him. Without grounding and orientating, you may decide to accept the ride home because you are caught up in the moment, even though isolating yourself with someone new is a big no-no in your personal protection strategy. Take a pause and look around the restaurant, naming what you can see and re-orientating yourself to your values and personal protection system. Then, politely decline. You bring yourself back into the present moment and do the safest thing. The safest thing is to wait until you know him better before getting into an enclosed space with him driving.

Using grounding and orientation will help you become more assertive in your communication style. When your consciousness is grounded in the present moment, you are better equipped to communicate your needs, wants, and desires. And when you are orientated to your surroundings, you will have more dialled-in situational awareness.

Resourcing

Resourcing is the practice of inviting your mind-body to attune to sensations of safety or goodness. It is a practice of invoking memories or thoughts in the present tense that give you a sense of ease, a sense of calm, and a feeling of 'okay-ness.'

In my yoga therapy classes, I might initiate your internal resourcing by asking you to follow along with a visualization technique or meditation. An example would be, "I invite you to let this now moment be enough. To be here right now. Allow yourself to feel a sense of ease, dropping the mind field away and breathing into your body. Feel the air pass through your nostrils, connect to the texture of the mat, and turn your ears down, quieting the noises around you right now."

> **Resourcing is the practice of inviting your mind-body to attune to sensations of safety or goodness.**

Resourcing can anchor your thoughts and sensations into the present moment and override the incessant pull of your mind. Remember that the goal of resourcing is to *invite the body-mind to sensations of safety and goodness*. It is a practice just like mindfulness! It creates positive samskaras and readily available, archived memories that our brains and nervous systems learn to rely upon. You can have positive and negative samskaras, much like there are positive and negative attributes to nervous system states. Samskaras are sophisticated groupings or impressions from past deeds and experiences.

Resourcing helps you eradicate the negative samskaras whilst developing positive ones. It is a lovely two for one impact exercise. This positive awareness of people, places, or things is stored in your memory bank and helps you override your negativity bias.

This somatic experiencing technique is wonderful for managing stress and can be done anywhere, anytime, and without any equipment. It also enables you to be in control of your well-being. By consciously directing your attention, you can merge the emotional brain with the rational brain, creating a synapse, if you will, to extinguish the stored fight/flight/freeze responses in the body. It is the conscious creation of feel-good energy! It can even become a habit that creates a positive samskara, or groove, by soothing the limbic system and the emotional brain. This is an important bridge in the body-mind: being able to soothe and bring relational wellness between the limbic system and the emotional brain.

Here are some simple steps to engage resourcing and bring sensations of safety and goodness to your body-mind:

1. Recall a positive, pleasant, feel-good memory.

2. Fill in all the details in your mind using as many senses as possible.

3. Use present tense to bring this into the body-mind!

4. The resource needs to be constructive and only have the feel-good elements in it.

5. Do not editorialize your resource by adding noise, traffic, aggravations, or anything negative.

6. The point is to elicit a feel-good feeling!

7. Give yourself a sense of 'okay-ness!'

8. Give yourself a sense of safety with your resources.

9. Talk to yourself in the first person as you recall this pleasant memory.

10. After you walk yourself mentally through your resource (by reciting in first person), come back to the sensation of your body.

11. Feel into your chair, feet, legs, arms, face, etc.

12. Notice your sensations, baseline breathing, throat, hands, neck, and shoulders.

Here is an example of one of my resources:

"I am walking with my dog Suki in the forest at Hidden Grove. I can feel the cool air of the rainforest and still have the taste of the oatmeal-chocolate chip cookie I ate on the way here in the car. Suki's white bum is wiggling off in the distance; she is doing her happy trot. I hear my water bottle sloshing at my hip as my feet hit the trail. I can sense Suki in the distance even though her cute white bum is out of sight."

You can use a memory from your past. It could be of a place; it could be of a person. Something that truly relaxes you and makes you feel joy is what you need for this to be a successful resourcing tool. Frame only the feel-good moments of your memory. If nothing readily comes to mind, if you have absolutely no feel-good memories, make one up and be as detailed as possible. But, if at all possible, recruit a real memory from your memory bank that is framed in the positive!

You are in control the whole time when you are resourcing! You can resource as often as you like. In fact, I recommend doing it frequently so you can create a positive imprint or samskara[32] that you can have at the ready! Resourcing will build up your confidence by knowing that you can direct your thoughts. You can change how you think and how you respond by resourcing consciously. When we go into our feel-good memory, our body will relax, just as when we are activated by something traumatic, our bodies tense up. Resourcing helps you build up the skill for positive noticing. For Resourcing to work, it must be constructive and not destructive. In order to regulate your nervous system, you want to develop conscious patterns to override the unconscious triggers! Even if you have a habit of dissociative behaviour when you become overwhelmed (like Ramani), bringing awareness to your behaviour is how you can change! For example, if you doom scroll or tune out by binge-watching Netflix to relieve stress, this is dissociative behaviour. And dissociative behavioural responses only relieve the fight/flight response temporarily. They do not let you settle into a rest and digest, liminal space. So, in the long run, those patterns of tuning out can be destructive to the process of repairing the nervous system. Resourcing helps your body interrupt the unconscious disorganization of your nervous system. It is a pattern interrupter! Build up a bank of constructive resourced memories that you can pull up any time stress and dysregulation threaten to interrupt your life.

Titration & Pendulation

Titration in somatic experiencing means to go slowly. Small, gradual additions over time. Titration will result in the gradual release of stored survival responses in the body. It recognizes that the body becomes compressed over time due to misused and unprocessed emotions. This compression leads to a prolonged state of contraction. You cannot

---

[32] Samskara is a Sanskrit word we use in the yogic traditions. It can be translated as an energetic pattern, a habit or pattern or a recollection. These energetic patterns exist in the unconscious level of our psyche and can create grooves or circuits in our nervous system. These grooves and patterns influence and affect our future actions much like the data that is in our autonomic nervous systems.

effectively discharge that energy all at once. This would completely overwhelm any person and prevent the successful reorganization of inputs for a healthy body-mind.

You need to understand that you have expansion/contraction cycles in response to stimuli and life's inputs. You get a new job and you are happy (expansive). You leave something familiar and you feel sad/ uncomfortable (contraction). You get recognized for an achievement and you feel appreciated (expansive). You are overstimulated from the attention (contraction). These are rhythmic cycles of life. Being able to process how those rhythmic cycles affect the individual in a slow, deliberate manner is how you heal the nervous system without overwhelming the individual.

In both of my teaching environments, whether I am teaching self-defence or yoga therapy, I titrate the experience for my students. I do not blast them with information, theory, exercises, and drills. I would never teach headstands in someone's first yoga class. Nor would I teach mounted, ground game scenarios in jiu-jitsu for a first class. We start slowly, gain momentum, back off, and re-approach.

> **When you go slowly and deliberately, you can see where you get stuck and how people, places, and things help or hinder you.**

With titration, you can more readily track advancement and identify where your hangups and hiccups are. When you go slowly and deliberately, you can see where you get stuck and how people, places, and things help or hinder you. One of our favourite sayings at Sadohana is "Slow is smooth, and smooth is fast." Invite this technique into your life. You can titrate your exposure to difficult inputs. You can titrate your exposure to the world by, for example, accepting some invitations and declining others. This is a method of protecting your peace and safety.

Titration is about learning how to take in information, process it bit by bit, back off, and re-approach it. It's learning how to add slowly, intentionally expanding your window of tolerance for interpersonal experiences, both for your input and output. Just like when you were a kid learning how to do life. You didn't just jump on the bike. You had someone hold the frame while you peddled, then you had training wheels, then you took off the training wheels. Titration is similar to this; you add slowly and take away when needed.

Now that we've covered titration, we will move on to pendulation. Pendulation is the natural, pulsatory phenomenon of expansion and contraction. You can think of pendulation like you would a pendulum. A pendulum is a suspended weight capable of swinging freely from a pivot. A pendulum can either move closer to or farther away from an object. Another way of saying this would be that the object can be expanded from the pendulum or contracted from the pendulum. You can use pendulation as a

You can use pendulation as a form of slowly moving towards something you traditionally avoid and then backing off into something you love.

form of slowly moving towards something you traditionally avoid and then backing off into something you love. For instance, pendulate into setting a boundary for when you will respond to emails or go on social media. If you prefer vacuuming over laundry, do laundry first, then vacuum. If you never pick where to go out for lunch but always pay, reverse it. Pendulate towards what you love. Expand your containment for anticipating good things. Expand your expectation that things will work out. Use pendulation to retreat into watching your show instead of doing the dishes. Use pendulation as a way to move towards things you usually avoid, as well as a way to expand towards things you love. When you are learning new things, start with something manageable. Do not tackle the hardest, most painful relationship you have in your life or try to influence boundaries right away. This is not an opportunity to grapple the big bucket items right out of the gate. This would be unwise and has the potential to blast your resources and leave you feeling discouraged. You must go slowly with implementing your new PEMS hygiene system and installing your new internal defence system!

Pendulation is a technique to employ when it serves you. Like most of the techniques presented in this book, if it doesn't serve you, it will create conflict and violence within. This is the opposite of healing and carefully constructing your new organizational system. Pendulation is a way you can approach something, be expansive, and then retreat and contract. Pendulation is a way to shift between states of discomfort and comfort and vice versa. You get to control this.

> **Embrace the ebb and flow, the expansion and contraction rhythm that is intrinsic to life.**

Your big takeaway right now is to embrace the ebb and flow, the expansion and contraction rhythm that is intrinsic to life. Do not beat yourself up and let your inner prosecutor say mean things when you are in a contraction cycle! No one is supposed to always be expanded! Embrace the moments in life when you can be expanded and accept the moments when you are contracted. Do not let that voice prosecute you when you are in a contraction cycle or take your shine down when you are in an expansion cycle. There is nothing wrong with you when you pendulate between these two cycles! You are not broken. Learn how to moderate your output by doing the things you can and then resting. Resist and retrain the tendency to burn out and retreat. You know that pattern, right? The hyper-independent behaviour style that has you taking on all the things and burning yourself out, forcing you to retreat and rest, only to return and repeat the cycle all over again.

Pendulation and titration support your nervous system's capacity to integrate highly charged inputs into a manageable rhythm. Backing off, going slow, anchoring your consciousness in the present moment, and embracing expansion and contraction are all part of your containment process. I hope you can see how these somatic experiencing techniques can be used as personal protection strategies. The more you learn how to manage your PEMS hygiene systems, the more readily available you are to the life you are carefully curating. Learning how to defend against gut punches gives you options, lessens the potential for violence, and breeds a safety state of mind. Resourcing gives you a readily available goodwill bank to make withdrawals from when you begin to feel overwhelmed. Resourcing is a prime self-soothing SE technique that interrupts the chemical pattern of dysregulation, creating positive neural pathways that you can rely upon. Grounding and Orientating is how you override patterns of rumination and anchor into safety. The autonomic nervous system has ingrained patterns that need to be rerouted so you do not continually lose yourself to feedback loops.

Being present has become more and more difficult with the incessant feed of stimuli coming at all of us, all the time, from everywhere. Using all of these SE techniques creates a new container for alternative routes so you can cease the reactivity cycles that cause dysregulation. Cultivating a safety state of mind so you can distinguish what is trauma and what is a gut instinct comes together through understanding containment. Expansion and contraction are the intrinsic, natural rhythm of this thing called life and living. At any time in life, we are either expanding or contracting. Something good happens, and you feel big. Expanded. Something bad happens, and you feel small. Contracted. With any body-based practice like skiing, pickleball, jiu-jitsu, yoga, pilates, etc., expansion and contraction will happen. New movement inputs can make you feel contracted, but once you achieve understanding and proficiency, you will feel expansive. Learning how to interpret and anticipate the ebb and flow of expansion and contraction is paramount to finding a sense of balance and acceptance in your life. Remember, we are biodynamic, electrical, quantum beings. We grow and shrink depending on inputs and outputs. Our entire body is a sophisticated network of organized inputs and outputs.

CHAPTER 17

Body Movement Practices

***I understand that this chapter heading can sound ableist.
I want to acknowledge that you may be someone who has
limited mobility, so I have five practices just for you to
try. Please know that I have a daughter who is mobility
challenged and that it takes tremendous trust to approach
movement with your body. Go easy dear heart!!*

Movement is medicine because moving the somatic sludge out of your tissues will heal you. Only movement will do. No amount of talk therapy will move the somatic sludge out of your tissues. We've already talked about somatic sludge, but I want to explore the topic a bit more in this chapter. Somatic sludge is the pervasive, whole-body sluggishness that spontaneously feels like your cells are breathing, expanding, and then contracting, all the while exchanging fuel and nutrients between them. Somatic sludge is the visceral feeling of your embodied self. Somatic sludge is an activating sensate presence, meaning it is an active apprehension of all the feeling senses in your body-mind, all at once. When you need to move, you can feel it. Dancing, walking, swimming, bike riding…these can be natural moments that you engage in regularly. You know the feeling when you are in your body, doing movements—

typically, you'll be able to shift a mental block when being active in this way. It may only be for the time you are engaged in movement, but a shift occurs nonetheless.

Most people who get injured have a decline in health because they stop moving and focus on the negative. They stay in the pain, in the fear of the pain, and in the restriction of movement. To heal from an injury, you have to reintroduce safe movement, and to heal somatic sludge, you have to move through the pain that constriction and injury cause. You have to train yourself to sit in the discomfort that limited movement causes and trust that it is not forever. You will change. The injury or setback is temporary. The somatic sludge can shift. The internal prosecutor will make you feel like shit and convince you that you are forever injured, broken, and less than. That voice is bullshit, and it takes feeling safe in your body again to teach you that that voice is bullshit. Healing from the inside out is rebuilding trust so you can listen to your gut instincts and implant tiny nuggets of faith. Faith that change is possible.

If you have mobility issues, these five body movement practices can be accomplished, irrespective of limitations.

1. **Whole Body Shaking**: You can stand or sit and shake the legs, the arms, and the fingers, roll into your joints, and safely lob your head from side to side. Shaking is what animals do in nature to discharge energy and dissipate stress. They shake to actualize their need for fight or flight. You can do the same. Set a timer for 30 seconds and shake. Do three sets with a five-minute break in between. Put some music on and shake your soma!

2. **Humming:** Hum with a closed mouth. Allow yourself to feel your own unique vibration and tone. Humming gives the mind something to focus on when it is in a ruminating cycle. Humming puts you into a rest and digest mode. You can certainly add chanting to this, but that can feel bold. I LOVE chanting, and I

LOVE humming. Play with the range of tone with your hum—go high, go low, have a gradual scale. Play with it! This is a gooder if you are out and about and need a regulation technique to use in public.

3. **Eye Movements:** This is a way to anchor your focus back into your body by consciously moving your eyes, not to be confused with Eye Movement Desensitization and Reprocessing (EMDR). EMDR is a specific psychotherapy treatment designed to alleviate distress associated with traumatic memories. It is a specific form of therapy with a trained practitioner, using protocols that guide the participant into memory sculpting with specific eye movements and other stimuli. The eye movements we're talking about are just moving your eyes, which is a simple yet incredible way to discharge energy and snap you back into presence.

TO DO Eye Movements: Move your eyes up to the ceiling, to the right, and to the left. Look down. Then look up again. Look rapidly from side to side. It can feel incredibly relaxing to pinball the eyes, side to side, after a big day. Close your eyes and rest in between your moments. You will be surprised how much stress you can let go of with eye movements. Lateral eye movements calm the nervous system because they quiet the amygdala. Practice panoramic vision, taking in the entirety of your view, as opposed to focal vision, which can be narrow. There is a reason we use phrases like 'Pan out and look at the whole picture.' Dilate your perception to see the world around you. Conversely, practice wakeful, deliberate disengagement with your field of vision, choosing what you focus on. There is a difference when you choose to focus your eyes on something, see the peripheral, or see the single point. Play with this!

4. **Breathwork**: There are so many prompts and practices for this. I will offer three.

    i.   Count your breaths, inhale for a count of four, and exhale for a count of three. Actually count them. When that feels comfortable, add a one-count pause at the end of the inhale and at the bottom of the exhale. It is important to state that far too many advanced breathing practices are given to people who do not have the nervous system stability to perform them. Instead of calming them down, breathwork can cause activation. Be very mindful with breath work and titrate new practices.

    ii. Bumblebee breath or blowing raspberries. Purse your lips together on exhale and blow a raspberry. You can add a buzzing sound as you do or just blow. The lips will vibrate and may even tickle. Do four rounds of raspberries, taking big enough inhales in between. This relaxes the face and jaw and moves you into a rest and digest mode. It is an active discharge of accumulative energy in your PEMS system.

    iii. Physiological Breath: Take two inhales and one exhale. This is a double inhale, one quick and one medium quick, then one longer exhale. The first inhale is a primer, and the second expands the lung sacs and pulls CO_2 out of the bloodstream. This breath can be used often. The Physiological Breath is one of the fastest ways to bring your ANS down to a regulated state.

5. **Gravity Anchor**: Consciously think about gravity being your friend. It is a force that pulls on your body. Feel into the pull of gravity and allow it to orientate you. What is up and what is down? Lean to the side, come away from your center line, with a limb, with your head. Then, move back into alignment with your

center line and connect to the pull that you feel from gravity. With a limb, move back, move forward, move side to side. Then, move back into alignment and feel supported by gravity. Anchor yourself into this trustworthy source.

Any of these somatic practices can be deployed to interrupt the emotional dysregulation cycle, which gives the body a chance to actualize and discharge alarms. and creates a feedback loop that changes the outcome of your behaviour. A feedback loop that fosters change and positive noticing, which gives you confidence to do it again the next time somatic sludge shows up. Whether or not you are familiar with yoga and jiu-jitsu, I encourage you to read what I have to say. These are my foundational practices, in which I employ all the somatic tools I have previously mentioned. There is so much available in these practices that often get overlooked by the commercialization and mainstream style of teaching.

Yoga Therapy

Individuals often have unhealthy habits of thinking bad, unhelpful thoughts or behaviours that undermine optimal healthy living. Humans like to drink, smoke, overeat, shop, avoid, and distract themselves. Yoga Therapy invites the individual to develop habits, deeds, and behaviours that make them feel good! It is a practice that supports inner discovery, safety, relaxation, and a sense of well-being. Practicing yoga therapy expands your consciousness away from survival mode and into rest and digest mode, which is when the parasympathetic branch of your nervous system is active. It is a practice that interrupts patterns of bad thoughts and mis-attunement. It invites your body into something other than the usual form, which, in itself, is supremely useful. Breaking patterns of dis-ease, misalignment, congestion, and constriction is how yoga therapy can create new neural pathways. You literally redesign the organizational structure of your body-mind by doing yoga therapy.

Repeating yoga poses builds new inputs in your body, as well as in your brain. You can get rid of the somatic sludge in your body-mind that prevents you from knowing your true self. The self that can live in bliss, pain-free, regulated, and engaged with people, places, and things. It is possible to work out the samskaras or pain points in your body. You can eliminate self-limiting beliefs. You could heal yourself. Yoga Therapy is not a cookie-cutter, 'Simon Says' type of yoga class that has become so popular in the West. Yoga Therapy deconstructs classical asanas[33] and incorporates mindful, synched breath-work[34] with meditative relaxation to bring balance to the body-mind. Instead of achieving an asana, in yoga therapy, you are experiencing the foundational principles of an asana. You don't just do tree pose; you re-distribute your body weight through the metatarsals, condition the ankles, lift out of the hips, relax, and tone the pelvic floor. Achieving a pose or asana is secondary in Yoga Therapy. Alleviating stress patterns in the body-mind is the goal. You learn how to hydrate fascia[35], strengthen stabilizer muscles, and discover how you manage load or weight bearing in your joints. This practice allows you to dip into both sympathetic output states (fight or flight) and restful parasympathetic states (rest and digest). Yoga and Yoga Therapy were designed to activate both branches of the autonomic nervous system and provide a whole-body reorganization for optimal well-being.

The first step in learning this body movement practice is recognizing where your body exists in space. Sensing where your body physically exists in space is called proprioception. In Yoga Therapy, you are discovering proprioception in simple and sophisticated ways. Self-inquiry as to which foot is my left foot and where my arms are in relation to my hips is simple

---

[33] Asana is the Sanskrit name for the poses performed in yoga class. They have been developed over the past 5000 years to heal the whole body-mind.

[34] Also called breath-control, the Sanskrit name for it is pranayama.

[35] Fascia is a connective tissue layer that surrounds and holds every organ, blood vessel, bone, nerve fibre, and muscle in place and is just as sensitive as skin. It responds to stress by tensing up, constricting, and becoming dense. As such, hydrating fascia is paramount to having a healthy body.

proprioception. Moving your right arm opposite to your left leg is a more sophisticated form of proprioception.

The second step, third step, and every step along the way as you move your body in a Yoga Therapy practice is listening to the inner landscape of the body. Being able to tune into what is happening inside the body is called interoception. It's feeling into the space of your spine, around your collarbones, and listening to the breath move into your left and right nostrils. Interoception is a scientific term for self-awareness. It is also incredible for healing the limbic system/emotional brain, as it asks you to interpret the inner language of the body. Interoception allows you to assign feelings to memories and to bring awareness to feelings. This practice interrupts the survival mode process. Interoception is a valuable tool that enables you to break default circuitry and patterns that grew out of certain survival states. Assigning feelings to memories and awareness to feelings releases stored survival stress. Bringing a deeper understanding of yourself to yourself is how you interrupt a pattern. This is how you heal. Identify what sets you off, recognize what makes you dysregulated, feel the feelings, move your body, hold the space, and interrupt the pattern of survival mode. This type of mindful, intentional inquiry restores gut instincts, strengthens awareness, stabilizes the mind on a single focus, and releases stored energy trapped in the muscles—by bringing your attention to the inner self.

Healing requires a witness. You must be that initial witness. When you unify where you exist in space (proprioception) with what you feel on the inside (interception), you create a bridge for uniting the rational and emotional sides of your psyche. Yoga Therapy upgrades your entire operating system and rebuilds your gut instinct for self-protection. Using yoga therapy to regulate the nervous system works because it is a multi-systems approach, factoring in physicality, emotional intelligence, avoidance, mental discernment, and effective communication, both within yourself and towards others. Yoga Therapy is the ultimate PEMS hygiene facilitator.

Yogis believe there is more to a person than just their body. The body is not just the sum total of a person's experience. The body encompasses all the feelings, emotions, memories, and timelines of your being in the present and generationally. When illness or dis-ease occurs, it is never just the physical body that needs attention. Yogis understood that our true nature is expansive and one of bliss. But the true self becomes obfuscated by the physical, energetic, and mental demands of life experience, interpersonal relationships, and generational timelines. The practice of yoga consists of self-discipline, awareness, and faith. This faith is in yourself, in the cosmos, and in source energy or God. This self-study/awarenessing underpins my whole philosophy of personal protection strategies. To know yourself means you can protect yourself from within as well as from without.

It is important to cultivate self-discipline to catch yourself when:

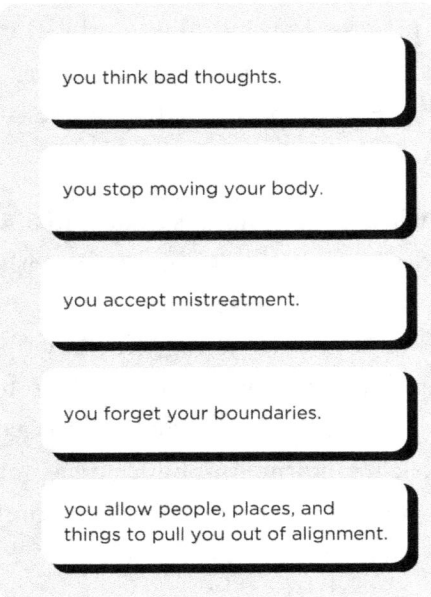

you think bad thoughts.

you stop moving your body.

you accept mistreatment.

you forget your boundaries.

you allow people, places, and things to pull you out of alignment.

Whether or not your consciousness is aware of it, bliss is always available. I know that can sound new age, impossible, or even insensitive if you have significant trauma. As someone who works relentlessly on healing her trauma, I can state with confidence that regardless of my personal stories and afflictions, bliss is always there, just beneath the surface. It is the natural state of being.

We, human beings, complicate our connection to bliss because we love to complicate most things. Blame our big brains. A shocking fact is that humans develop complex attachments to pain, contraction, dis-ease, and addiction and form maladaptive coping mechanisms early on. It is not our fault. When your core needs have been violated, impacted, or influenced—from inception onwards—this causes misalignment to stress cues. Your ability to self-soothe gets disrupted over and over again until you can interrupt that organizational structure and learn how to self-soothe in a healthy way, discharge the stored survival stress, and learn what your personality is outside of the coping mechanism.

Through a lifetime of cultural influences, family dynamics, repeated stress patterns in your body, and trauma, you will develop a nervous system that responds unconsciously to the world around you. If the body is under constant strain, the nerve highways can become inhibited, and the organization of inputs becomes disrupted. Chronic pain, joint issues, and misalignment will create contracted states in the body, restricting full range of motion. This causes contraction in how you regulate hormones, which affects the mental well-being of the individual. Contracted states of being lead to anxiety, depression, and dysregulation.

When clients seek me out for yoga therapy sessions, we start with what they show up with. Invariably, our professional relationship begins because they have injured themselves. They are only concerned with the body part that has stopped functioning for them. Mostly, they are overworked, overtaxed, and out of whack with sleep, metabolism, and peer to peer connection. Unwittingly, they have fractured their own core needs for connection, attunement, trust, autonomy, and love/sexuality through an imbalance of work-life dynamics. They have denied the cues the body-mind initially whispered to them, compounding insult with injury until the body-mind breaks down. They can no longer ignore a certain body part. So, they seek out a practice to bring balance and healing back to their body. They intuitively know that they want more harmony and bliss, and simple physio exercises are not enough.

My client, Mark, came to me after doing physio for eight months. He said one of the biggest gifts of working with me was that I customized the class for him. I stood with him the entire time a new movement was initiated and corrected imbalances on the spot. Mark was able to employ proprioception and interoception because he had a coach guiding him into the body as he moved. During his physio sessions, he would be given the exercises and then left to complete them on his own. There was a little bit of instruction, but he remarked that the biggest difference was that the movement inputs I gave him were managed step by step. We did not just focus on the injured part of his body but the accompanying parts as well because the body only works as a whole. It is an integrated cosmos that affects each and every part. When Mark would identify the individual holding patterns that caused wear, strain, and stress in his body, he could interrupt his movements so they supported his well-being. Having the discipline to practice is the hardest part. Mark was able to be witnessed every time he stepped on the mat. This led him to discover all the other parts of his PEMS hygiene system that were out of whack.

When I talk about contracted stress patterns, I want you to imagine a garden hose that has been coiled all winter. In springtime, you go to uncoil the hose, but it snaps back into the hibernation pattern. You uncoil it, get the water running, and hold tension in the line so you can use the hose, but as soon as you turn off the water and let go of the hose, the hose will recoil to its habituated, nesting state. The human body responds the same way. It takes consistent and deliberate movement, linked with mindful breath work, reflective inquiry, and time to re-establish a new pattern that embraces the expansion, welcomes the unfolding, and installs supportive, holistic inputs. Yoga Therapy, in its essence, is a personal protection skill. It teaches you how to have faith, expand your body-mind, and return to safety.

Jiu-Jitsu

The reason why jiu-jitsu is so good at healing trauma is because it increases your window of tolerance for uncomfortable situations, provided you are training in a SAFE school, academy, or dojo with trauma-informed instructors. Jiu-jitsu is indiscriminate in asking everyone to subject themselves to uncomfortable situations. Whether you are grabbing someone's wrist, doing solo floor drills, practicing knee on belly, or performing a full mount, you will feel uncomfortable and wish for the action to cease. Jiu-jitsu provides a safe space to handle a physical load of pressure with bodies on top of bodies. You are presented with a real-time, physical limitation, and you have to problem-solve your way out of it!

Healing trauma invites you to move past the rigidity of your mind-body. When you become more adaptable to people, places, and things, your window of tolerance expands, and you reduce the rigidity in your mind-body. When I use the word adaptable, I do not mean adjusting to levels of abuse. I mean adaptability in changing how you respond to difficult or triggering inputs.

Jiu-jitsu comes from the Japanese word jujutsu, which can be broken into ju, meaning gentle, yielding, and flexible, and jutsu, meaning art or technique. The lineage of jiu-jitsu comes directly from the Samurai class. A class of people who lived Budo[36]: a life of honour, discipline, and consistency. Jiu-jitsu has become popular through Mixed Martial Arts (MMA) style fighting, notably, the UFC. The most popular form of jiu-jitsu right now is Brazilian jiu-jitsu or BJJ. BJJ focuses primarily

---

[36] Budo is a Japanese word that means "martial way" or "the way of the warrior."

on ground control, grips, and positional dominance and is practiced in
a Gi and No-Gi (wearing rash guards or spats). Though I practice both,
my real love is in the stand-up, self-defence-orientated Japanese jujutsu
(JJJ). This is mostly because I have practiced it longer and am, frankly,
more skilled at JJJ than BJJ. There is a slight difference in the spelling
of Jiu-Jitsu or Jujutsu. The latter refers to Japanese styles, whereas the
former was coined in the 20ᵗʰ century and encompasses both Japanese
and Brazilian jiu-jitsu. Just so you know, I will use them interchangeably.

Jujutsu literally means 'the gentle art.'

Jujutsu literally means 'the gentle art.' It
uses leverage as the foundational principle.
Jiu-jitsu can be done by anyone, regardless
of age or body type, provided you are with
the right school, academy, or dojo.[37] By
using leverage, base, stance, and yielding,
it does not matter your size; you can practice jiu-jitsu effectively. There
is the physicality of jiu-jitsu, such as the warm-up, cardio, and agility
aspects, which will test you. Then there is the mental aspect: having the
presence of mind to willingly submit to pressure. The spiritual aspect is
to have the humbleness to dig deep within and try and try again to drill
a technique and receive your desired outcome. Emotionally, it can feed
you or deplete you, depending on what is going on in your world, but
ultimately, you always leave the mat feeling better than when you got on
it.

The three main advantages of doing jiu-jitsu to heal trauma are:

1. You get to move your body in ways that are both new and
    possibly related to a traumatic experience where you did not
    know how to move your body. For example, learning how to
    execute a knee shield from a side position so someone cannot

---

[37] Dojo is the Japanese word for "the place of the way." It is primarily the practice hall for
martial arts. In the same way a studio is where one practices yoga, a dojo implies a place to
practice Jujutsu.

get into your guard (between your legs and on top of you) is an amazing drill to perform, helping you reclaim your power and giving you confidence that you are in control. Moving your body in new ways creates new inputs, which translates to change.

2. It expands your window of tolerance for stressful experiences. Just getting on the mat can feel stressful. Even I still feel stress when I know I am about to willingly put myself in uncomfortable positions that I have to navigate out of. By expanding your window of tolerance, your resilience increases. You become resilient to new levels of stress, new levels of pressure, and new experiences with training partners. This is invaluable when dealing with difficult people, places, and things off the mat.

3. You get to engage in a social community that supports your growth. Everyone on the mat wants you to succeed and level up. Your training partners are invested in your success because when you level up, and they level up, your training becomes magical together.

In jiu-jitsu you are learning new inputs, managing pressure, finding space, getting stuck, regulating your breath, and looking for positional dominance, release, and completion. It is a wonderful metaphor for what is needed to succeed at life! If you have ever been pinned down by an older brother or held against your will, you will have a stored survival response of being trapped. Being able to move your body and complete the escape helps discharge the stored survival stress that was created by the past event of not being able to complete the escape. You get to have agency over your body after it may have been tampered with, which is why jiu-jitsu is so incredible to practice. You can confront your triggers in real time with safe training partners and rewire your nervous system to successful completion. You get to de-stigmatize what it feels like to have someone on top of you or pinning you down and discharge the stored trauma response out of your tissues.

I do not like it when someone grabs my arm or my hand forcefully. I get incredibly uncomfortable with people in my personal space. So, I get it if you are reading this and thinking, "Fuck no! None of this sounds therapeutic." I got you. It takes time, but leaning into this practice can benefit you in many, many ways. Every day on the mat, you have to find comfort while being extremely uncomfortable. Jiu-jitsu is learning how to live in the suck. It does not discriminate. Everyone has to learn how to embrace the suck, but there is great value in learning how to do so.

In contrast to yoga therapy, where you are on the mat by yourself, getting cues to move your body, in jiu-jitsu, you have to move your body AS WELL as someone else's! You have to be present and mindful so you don't injure yourself or your partner.

At my school, Sadohana, our Japanese system is called KoKoDo[38] Jujutsu (KKD JJ). We tap into an ancient energy system that has been cultivated and refined for the pursuit of personal protection, developed by Soke Irie Yasuhiro, a direct descendant of the samurai class. In KKD JJ, we play with concepts of spirals, off-balancing, neutralization, elevation, and angles. Being able to move the body from the inside out is how you succeed in gaining access to the higher Dans (levels) of this art. Soke wants your technique to be devastating AND beautiful. Moving the body efficiently, with grace and fluidity, is a hallmark of this style.

When I was leveling up to Menkyo Kaiden (6th Dan, Licensed, Master Instructor with full transmission), I found the training to be exceptionally challenging and mind-bending. During one training session, for example, I was asked to move the energy in my body so I could affect my opponent. My sensei[39] asked me to imagine "I was a bathtub filled with water". He told me not to let the water touch either side of my imaginary bathtub. Huh? I give you this example to illustrate the mental, physical, spiritual, and emotional considerations you can be initiated into as you advance

---

[38] KoKoDo means "Imperial Light Way"

[39] Japanese term for teacher.

in training this martial art. Every time you practice a waza, your aim is to transfer energy, adjust your body weight so you can move efficiently, use precise angles, correct elevation, and appropriate distance between you and the opponent. In KKD JJ, you wear a full Gi: pants, top, and belt. When you get a black belt, you wear a Hakama, a fabulous, pleated, wide-legged pant, over your Gi pants or shorts. It is a very regal outfit that comes from the Samurai in Japanese culture. Every time I get suited up for class, I feel the ceremony of the uniform, preparing my mind-body for class.

Just like yoga therapy, the art of jiu-jitsu invites you to rewire your brain and your internal defence system. It interrupts the regular programming of output and input. It allows you to engage in movement inputs that are not your regular sitting, driving, walking, or running. However, unlike yoga therapy, it is not a solo practice; you need a training partner. Having someone you can co-regulate with is amazing. Co-regulation can be as simple as being able to mutually discharge the stresses of the day together. There does not need to be a significant event that occurs on the mat for you to co-regulate with someone. Just synching breathing patterns together is amazing. This type of co-regulation allows you to access and soothe your core needs for connection, attunement, trust, and autonomy.

Learning how to protect your physical boundaries and your physical body in jiu-jitsu will give you confidence that translates off the mat. I do not want you to envision a combative, sport-type style of jiu-jitsu. You are not training so you can fight in a competition with others. That is not what I am recommending for healing your trauma. In a trauma-informed dojo, you will work both floor drills and stand-up drills, and you will be able to titrate your experience, learning new inputs gradually. You need an instructor who can safely bring you into new experiences with jiu-jitsu. You should be able to trust those who have gone before you, expand your window of tolerance, and back off and re-approach your practice with a community of people who want to support you. A dojo family can sometimes be way better than the family you were born with. At the very least, they can be a wonderful addition.

I happen to be married to my jiu-jitsu teacher, Michael Seamark, Hanshi. We have been able to heal together, and I know that by showing up as my neuro-spicy self, I have brought a new level of education and awareness to our academy and school. It is no small thing to train with your husband and leave the kids, laundry, chores, and domestic life out of the dojo. Thankfully, I married someone who is just as committed to personal growth and healing as I am, so we have not only made it work but we've also made it something beautiful. Our dojo is an extension of our love language.

A true trauma-informed Sensei will be able to pick up on cues and subtleties that foretell how to proceed. This is how you can train safely and, most importantly, invite safety back to yourself. The instructors at Sadohana have learned how to read unsafe cues, meaning they can read body language and anticipate when someone gets overstimulated or activated.

Just a few months ago, while training, my husband saw my eyes go glassy and felt the shift in my energy from engaged to shutdown. He gave me permission to step off the mat and go into my office. I was going to muscle through and go through the motions. This hyper-independent side of me is a front for my abandonment wound—it is a form of self-abandoning that I use to cope with my fear of being abandoned by others. This self-abandonment reads as stoicism and was programmed into me by the women in my family. They all justified external output, even to their own detriment. Their motto was just to keep going, to get it done, and even deny your feelings and emotional well-being if necessary, as long as you get the job done and show up for other people. Certainly, never show up for yourself and ask for things! That was the message I received that got pre-loaded into my autonomic nervous system. Being given permission to leave the mat and, more importantly, having my teacher anticipate what I could not grant myself was a game changer. Learning the language of nervous system regulation, coupled with my movement practices, is how I learned to heal my trauma from the inside out. Meaning I can experience life outside of survival mode!

So, what happens if I train with someone who doesn't know me well? I inform them of my boundaries, and I choose training partners who I believe will respect those boundaries. I will tell them that if I say stop, they must stop. I do not let them invade my space. I run quicker repetitions so I can assimilate the mechanics of a technique without having to bear a major load or be subjected to too much pressure. Pressure, being mounted, and chokes are my albatross, my kryptonite. In BJJ, between rounds or reps, I will stand up and shake—shake my body and flick my hands and fingers. I will lie down, knees bent, feet planted, and then rock my knees side to side and roll my head side to side. I will sit out and watch. I will put my legs up the wall in the corner of the dojo. I will disengage and orientate myself, release the build-up, and use my breath to anchor myself. Training is a great place to make use of the somatic experiencing technique of titration. You are always in control of your training on the mat.

In KKD, I will sit out and observe when needed. Luckily, at my level of training, there are more minutiae in the execution of the techniques and less dynamic throws or falls. This enables me to work in bite-size pieces, re-working a principle or technique over and over again before moving on.

Knowing that I could have an episode of dissociation while training helps my training because it has happened already, and I didn't stop training. It helps me to regulate my inner child's core wounds, my unconscious, and my shadow self. How? Because I know I have already been triggered badly on the mat, and I survived. As your window of tolerance expands, you can anchor your consciousness in what is happening in real time more and more. You cease being overrun with emotional flashbacks and the accompanying dissociation. You will be able to tell yourself that you are okay, and in time, it will be true. When you meet the uncomfortable bits that feeling your feelings brings and expand your container, you too, can reassure yourself that you can handle what the body-mind has to share. This is empowered healing!

Healing is the ability to connect to the people, places, and things around you.

Being able to move beyond your own limiting beliefs about healing and self-defence is what this book is empowering you to do. Whether or not you use yoga, Wim Hoff breathing, cold plunges, fasting, or Tai Chi, ultimately, you are taking steps not just to heal but to be able to connect. This is what healing is: the ability to connect to the people, places, and things around you. This connection comes from updating your operating system and soothing unmet needs for connection, love, trust, autonomy, and attunement. This is how you not only succeed but learn to thrive: Using movement as medicine with trusted, trauma-informed instructors. Use movement to nurture your PEMS hygiene system, find the patterns of dysregulation, and reorganize your internal inputs to support and return yourself back to safety from the inside out.

CHAPTER 18

Recapitulation

Recapitulation is a self-awarenessing technique inspired by ancient Toltec practices that focuses on using the nervous system to heal through body remembering. Before I teach you how to do recapitulation, allow me to give you the backdrop of my immersion into a community of women healers and why and how this technique became a mainstay in my PEMS hygiene management.

In the fall of 1999, my husband and I were coming home from a yoga nidra workshop my friend Wade Imre Morissette was hosting. We were travelling on Lion's Gate Bridge to get back to North Van when we were struck in a head-on collision that tore off the driver's side of our car. We were saved by my quick thinking to crank the wheel to the right, minimizing the impact just enough to avoid certain death. Our car was spun 2 times in 360 degrees before we skidded to a stop, avoiding a secondary impact from the cars behind us. My husband, seeing we were still in danger, pulled me from the car, which was amazing, considering the car had compacted around my form. I was driving, and the metal held my foot as if in a case, but adrenaline can do miraculous things. He freed me, and we got out of the car as the crash scene continued. The firemen on the scene couldn't believe we were in the car and concluded that we were either very lucky or very hurt and just didn't know it yet. All things considered, we were very lucky.

Our twin babies were not in the car, thankfully, as the back seat where their car seats were was covered in shards of glass. We were also very hurt in a way that was deceptive. I walked away with soft tissue injury, spinal herniation, and nerve damage. Walking away being the primary! The thing with soft tissue injury and nerve damage, however, is that it lingers and flares for decades afterwards. You are not in a full body cast, and nothing is broken, so you have this false sense of wellness that only time can correct.

I had been doing Gabrielle Roths' 5Rhythms dance after the birth of our twins to reacquaint myself with my new body. I was no longer nursing, and my body felt like it was mine again after two years of renting it out to carry, birth, and nurture babies. During one of the dance workshops, I met some wonderful women who happened to live on Pender Island, a gulf island just southwest of the mainland where I lived at the time. After the head-on collision, knowing I needed more support in my healing, I reached out to them, and within a week, they secured me a cabin on a lake and weekly bodywork sessions. I had just gotten back to work, teaching yoga again and doing jiu-jitsu when the car crash happened. So here I was in incredible pain, bedridden to reduce the load on my spine so as not to inflame the already overloaded nerves and discs, with 13-month-old twins who had just found their legs and were crawling and walking everywhere!

By the grace of God, these women appeared to help me heal.

> **By the grace of God, these women appeared to help me heal.**

One of them in particular, Kim Reschke, whom I met doing the 5Rhythms Dance workshop (and who instigated the whole transplant to Pender Island), was an incredible medicine woman, physiotherapist and aspiring Shaman. She taught me the recapitulation technique. She gave profound healing sessions, blending psycho-spiritual wound healing with skeletal and muscle adjustments. She guided me on how to reclaim my lost energy so I could fully heal from the impact of the car crash and find liberation from the negative interactions that were blocking me.

My sessions with Kim were life changing and enabled me to resume teaching and living my life with containment. By the spring of 2000, I taught my first hybrid women's self-defence program with yoga therapy on Pender Island in this community. We were all new mothers, and we were all seekers and self-healers of different backgrounds and professions. We gave one another permission to explore wisdom, knowledge, healing, and developmental practices.

This community of women healers, who facilitated so much of my recovery from the severe motor vehicle accident, reminds me of who I imagine the Toltecs were (we'll get to that in a bit). Bringing self-defence to a community of healers meant I had to break down the conditioning that exists in our society around self-defence and personal protection strategies. I had to show this remarkable group of women how to bring their femininity to this predominantly masculine endeavour and how to feel safe doing so. There is a vast cultural programming that self defence is a manly-man sport that uses brute force and aggressive tactics to defend oneself. One of the biggest myths I see perpetuated in self defence classes and books is the readily available level of aggression used to execute techniques, with zero counsel on the emotional deficit required.

Let me explain. I am sure you have seen the ads promising to teach you "How to gouge a man's eyeballs out!" "How to disable an attacker with three moves!" or "Aim for the groin and run." Okay, that last one is effective, but it is so important to KNOW when to strike. You should refrain from punching or kicking if possible. It can go badly very quickly if you do not have any training. If you must hit, use it as a distraction so you can get away.

My issue with that style of self-defence teaching (only focussing on the physical aspect of self-defence) is that it has a hyper-masculine quality when a more nuanced understanding of the whole body-mind is imperative. It is nauseating to continually equate emotional intelligence as a predominately feminine quality, but alas, that is still a culturally sanctioned truth as of 2025. One that hopefully changes as men are allowed and encouraged to develop their own robust PEMS hygiene system. I will add that I am blessed to be around quite a few high-calibre, emotionally adept men in our jiu-jitsu community in Vancouver.

This last practice in this book that I am giving you is one more technique to add to your PEMS hygiene toolkit. It is a way to release yourself from the grooves of the past into a pattern for exploratory expansion like the ancient Toltecs once did. The term recapitulation was first coined in print by Carlos Castaneda,[40] who was an anthropologist, author, and teacher who wrote about mastering awareness. If you have been wondering who and what a Toltec is, allow me to offer this explanation from renowned spiritual teacher and internationally bestselling author Don Miguel Ruiz.[41] In his book, *The Mastery of Love*, he gives us this description of what a Toltec is:

> *"Thousands of years ago, the Toltec were known throughout southern Mexico as 'women and men of knowledge.' Anthropologists have spoken of the Toltec as a nation or race, but in fact, the Toltec were scientists and artists who formed a society to explore and conserve the spiritual knowledge and practices of the ancient ones."*

---

[40] In the book, *The Eagles Gift*. New York: Pocket Books, 1982

[41] Don Miguel Ruiz also wrote the widely acclaimed book *The Four Agreements*, which was published in 1997 and has sold over 10 million copies in the United States alone.

Every interaction you experience in life has the potential to leave trapped energy in the body, creating samskaras, or timelines, that shape who you are as an individual. For me, it was not just the head-on collision but the exchange I had with the firefighters and ambulance attendants that needed to be cleared. It wasn't just the impact but the lingering damage from the doctors, the emergency room, and the stop-and-start healing that I needed to learn how to clear. Excavating samskaras and healing stored pain points will release energy that keeps you stuck and keeps you moving in cyclical patterns that create ruts for your potential power.

This is where Recapitulation shines.

Recapitulation involves a systematic review of your life, pinpointing an event, person, place, or thing that had an emotional charge. The body keeps score and remembers everything, even when the mind does not.

This is where Recapitulation shines.

By reclaiming the energy, you release its charge, free the stored alarm/trapped pain response associated with it, and free yourself of the samskara time stamp.

The purpose of recapitulation is to reclaim, recover, and release trapped energy. It is something that you must feel as opposed to think about. Freeing stored survival responses will give you back agency. Reclaiming your energy will give you energy. But in all likelihood, it will feel foreign, weird, and scary to start.

Get ready and go easy!

Relieving your body and mind from congestion by offering completion and autonomous verbal ventilation is what makes recapitulation so powerful. You may recall in the chapter on self-abandonment we spoke about how autonomous verbal ventilation is speaking out loud to yourself, to a voice note on your phone, kvetching with a friend, or just speaking out into the ether of the universe to release trapped energetic signatures.

As an example of a simple, innocuous exchange that happens in your everyday life, consider this: Have you ever had a dispute with a friend or a stranger and found that, for days or weeks afterwards, you continued to play out the scenario? The *would've, could've, should've* reactivity loop in your mind? This loop, or mental ruminating tape recorder, drains your energy and your prana.[42] Now imagine the bigger life events you have experienced and couple them with the day-to-day events, and you can see how they are lodged in that mental, energetic tape recorder that amasses into a wall-to-wall record shop of stored undelivered communications.

This technique is designed to call back the energy that has been trapped by a specific event, person, place, or thing and bring you freedom and ease! It is meant to release you from the ruminating mental tape recorder and clear away any debris in your nervous system highways. Doing recapitulation is something that you can do forever. Some events themselves may need multiple recapitulation sessions to effectively release the charge and reclaim the trapped energy. Again, reflect on how long an unvoiced core need or experience can stay in your psyche. Recapitulation allows you to consciously revisit these episodes of unmet core needs or disputes and release the charge they have over you. Recapitulation is a PEMS supercharger for not only the big ones, like the motor vehicle accident I was in, but also the everyday life exchanges that take up a surprising amount of PEMS cargo when left unchecked.

Disclaimer Before I Teach You the Technique!

Remembering hurtful, charged, negative, or traumatic events will bring with them emotions and feelings that could feel overwhelming. When recalling something fearful or highly charged, the brain and nervous system will respond just like it is happening all over again. Being forewarned is being forearmed and is an integral part of your preparation strategy in self-defence. You will need time to process, integrate, and rest when you

---

[42] Prana is the Sanskrit word for life force or breath in the body.

are using this tool. In other words, do not slot a 15-minute recapitulation session in before you have to go to work or pick the kids up from school. Pad your session with recovery time. You can do a recapitulation session and then rest with music or a show or a nap or a bath, whatever it is that you use to help yourself regulate and transition from an activated state to a neutral state. Sitting or lying down in stillness—BEING in the liminal space of not DOING—will help increase your containment for re-visiting highly charged events. It is in the liminal space that teaches your nervous system that it can be safe and in control.

Disclaimer guidelines:

▸▸ Always start with something small and manageable.

▸▸ Know that you can stop at any time should you feel overwhelmed.

▸▸ You are always in control of this!

▸▸ Never start with big T trauma events.

▸▸ Your systems can get overloaded very quickly.

▸▸ You are in training.

▸▸ You can build up to the bigger items after you start small, with little events and memories.

How to Do Recapitulation

Recapitulation is performed using coordinated breath work, subtle head movements, and visualization in a safe space, preferably with a heavy blanket. Recruit the somatic experiencing techniques you have learned, namely resourcing and titration. Resourcing is having feel-good vibes and glimmers in your mind palace bank, to help you self-regulate your nervous system if you get overwhelmed by the sensations of recapitulating. Your mind palace bank is a phrase to enrich your agency over how you think about thinking and to encourage you to think about your mind having a safe place, with good memories and feel good glimmers. Titration means to go slowly, add and subtract. Enter into this exercise slowly, with low vibe interactions. Start with a little t event or other stored survival response (injury, medical intervention, argument, etc.) and build up your window of tolerance before you move forward. Take as much time as you need. You will be surprised to find out what samskaras have latched onto your energetic field and how long they've been there. Even something you may have perceived as incidental or of no consequence can burrow into your energetic field.

The goal is not only to free your body of trapped negative energy and gain power but also to learn how to regulate your own nervous system by discharging the reactivity cycle. Learning how to revisit painful, activating, triggering, or higher voltage memories whilst being in control of the now moment is what will recreate safety within yourself and build up your instincts for self-protection. Revisiting and then resting in the liminal space between actions is key. Being in control of releasing the charge of these memories breeds confidence and self-assurance. Please do not fret; you cannot do this wrong.

Instructions

(I will use the term *event* as the catchall for stored survival response, traumatic memories, and the people, places, or things that you are recapitulating.)

The goal is to remember specific events in your life that have had an impact, have left you with undelivered communications, or injured you in some way. This can be an actual injury or an energetic injury. Having had a person, place, or thing impact your emotional well-being in some way is an event that you can process.

You can practice this exercise many times. In fact, I recommend that you do.

Remember: Start with something small. It is also easier to start with something recent so you can evoke all the sense memories of sight, touch, smell, thought, feeling, place, and things, bringing the mind back to the event in as much detail as possible.

You can use Recapitulation for many different types of exchanges or situations. Here are a few for you to consider:

- ▶▶ Difficult or awkward exchanges between friends and family
- ▶▶ Past holidays that were weird or uncomfortable
- ▶▶ Exchanges with co-workers
- ▶▶ Death of a pet
- ▶▶ Power imbalance from a friend
- ▶▶ A personal overshare
- ▶▶ Unwanted knowledge of gossip
- ▶▶ Rude exchange with a stranger
- ▶▶ Past injuries, surgeries, or accidents
- ▶▶ Past lovers

*If you have difficulty articulating specific negative events, you can use this as your template. If you do not feel safe in your body to recollect something specific, that is absolutely okay. Start with this: "I want to release this," and breathe out as you turn your head from facing right to facing left. Leave it ambiguous and continue with six repetitions of "I want to release this," and breathe as you turn your head from right to left.

Take your time and feel into this technique; you cannot do it wrong. Find the rhythm and breath pattern that feels best for you.

Here is the sequence:

1. **Schedule a time for you to recapitulate.** This guideline uses 30 minutes.

2. **Use five to eight minutes to write out your event.** Make a list of the event in bullet points. Include sensations of what you see, smell, hear, think, and feel to recall the energy of the event.

3. **Use these prompts to recall the event:**

    a.   Where am I?

    b.   What am I wearing?

    c.   How do I feel?

    d.   What can I smell?

    e.   Who do I see around me?

    f.   What am I thinking?

    g.   What happened?

4. **Lie down or sit comfortably.** Have a blanket or pillow for support. Using a blanket for warmth and also for comfort gives you a tactile sensation, reassuring, like a hug to yourself. Take two minutes to get settled after writing out your event.

5. **Read the list, one bullet point at a time.** Spend ten minutes saying the bullet items and breathing your head from side to side.

6. **Turn your head to the right when you read the bullet point.** Once read, take a breath and turn your head to the left.

7. **Continue reading and moving your head right to left as you read the rest of your bullet points.** Don't worry if synching the breath is not right; just remember to breathe in and

out after speaking and while moving your head. This is for you to adapt and make your own.

8. **If a particular bullet point is more charged than others, re-read it, moving your head from right to left until you feel your baseline return to normal.** Until the charge is released. There is no need for self-judgement or recrimination; you may be surprised what part of the event has the most charge when you revisit it.

9. **Once you have read through your list, finish your session with an all-inclusive: "I release foreign energy left and return it back to the source."** I find this helps gather any bits I could not put into words and release the energy.

10. **Give yourself eight to ten minutes to be in a non-thinking space.** You can also resource, nap, cry, or self-soothe. You can play music and just sit with the after-effects, allowing your nervous system to regulate in peace and calm. This is important! After the verbal ventilation, recollection, and reliving to discharge the event, you want to allow your energy to come back to homeostasis. This is training your nervous system to find regulation after stimulation. This is being in liminal space. You are in control of this at all times.

Here is an example of a negative event that left a charge. This is an innocuous event, something that had a little charge for me, just enough to trip me up. This is the kind of example you should start with. Build up from here!

I am at the grocery store, waiting in line.

I am wearing a cute spring outfit, toenails just painted, in my Japanese sandals.

I feel calm and accomplished, and a little bit cold as the air conditioning is on.

I can smell a big box, supermarket smell.

Around me I see check-out clerks and other customers.

I am thinking about not cooking dinner after this and ordering sushi. I am mentally compiling a sushi order.

An impatient, rude man behind me starts muttering under his breath, catches my eye, asks me if I could take any longer, and calls me a bitch as he looks down and aggressively shoves his cart close to me.

I am confused as to why this is happening and also annoyed.

I go to a different till, but he follows me there.

I park my grocery cart and tell the clerk I need something else, and I tell him he can go ahead. He says finally, no thank you, and goes ahead.

I move down an aisle, where there are other clerks stocking shelves.

I can feel my heart beating hard and fast, and I feel my hands are warm and sweaty on my purse.

I am disappointed, angry, and bewildered that this happened and ready to go home. I suddenly feel tired but also energized and alert.

Once the angry man is finished checking out, I go back to my cart.

The clerk who checks me out is super nice and pleasant and remarks on how nice it is that the weather is getting warmer.

I say I agree and do not mention the unpleasant encounter as I see the rude, impatient man leave the store.

I pack up my groceries and head to the elevator, in the opposite direction entirely from the impatient man (he went to the front of the store, and I am going up to the open parkade), feeling determined to finish grocery shopping, discharge the bad vibes from the impatient man and eager to call in my sushi order.

Recapitulation will aid in healing your nervous system because you will be reclaiming lost energy from undelivered communications and releasing stored survival responses from people, places, and things in a deliberate, thoughtful way that gives you back your power. Nerves that wire together, fire together. Doing this technique allows you to knit back your entire PEMS hygiene system, repatterning your circuitry to serve you rather than defeat you.

Conclusion

Did you think it was weird to talk about self-defence in a book about healing trauma? Most people shy away from self-defence because they think it is about fighting, and people have a hard enough time setting boundaries, let alone thinking about a throat punch. Most people reject the notion that they may have trauma because it is a word that has become overused and weaponized. The fact remains, you have received a series of wounds simply by the nature of being a human in this world. How you respond to stimuli depends on how healthy your primary wiring was growing up.

Trauma is not just the big T events. Trauma occurs through illness, accidents, loss, and rejection. Trauma is a stored or trapped survival response, and it changes how your intuition perceives the world around you. Left unaddressed, you confuse your personality with the faulty feedback loop of your nervous system, responding to perceived threats and accepting a baseline of dysregulated behaviour. Remember the guy who chased me with gardener snakes? It took me years to figure out that it was my stored survival stress punching me in the gut and that not everyone with his name was bad!

It makes people uncomfortable to anticipate potential violence. Women, in particular, are cursed with default, nice girl programming, so they learn from an early age to ignore their gut instincts, put others' needs first, self-abandon, gaslight themselves, and try not to take up space. For decades my healing and self-defence journey was a confusing onslaught of mismanaged emotions and intentions. I would make progress and then regress substantially. I was always looking for that one thing that would fix all the things. I had to learn that I needed a multi-systems approach. I created the PEMS hygiene system to be that multi-directional system that will help you break out of survival mode.

It taught me:

1. how to create safety in my body.
2. how to have grace and joy in my life.
3. how to heal the issues in my tissue.
4. how to have healthy boundaries.
5. how to reparent my parentified self.
6. how to celebrate all the ways somatic sludge shows up.

One of the benefits of growing up with extreme abuse is that I am not ignorant of and do not pretend that people are not capable of what I know people are capable of doing. Predators are rarely lurking in the bushes as much as they are a person already known to you, waiting for their opportunity to advance. There are bad people in this world who will try to hurt you. Violence is a reality, not your responsibility. I have armed you with situational awareness tools and a threat cues checklist and taught you how to use code words or phrases. These strategies are part of how you create your safety state of mind. I've shown you how there is an arc or varying degrees to which someone can impact you. From a regular person with unconscious patterns to a premeditated predator. Unconscious patterns will wear you down in the same way that people can trespass into your energy and siphon or deplete your resources.

Using the PEMS hygiene system, your mind cannot get bored or convince you to stay stuck or be comfortable in the familiar patterns that hurt you. Reclaiming lost energy from past events will give you power and help you complete undelivered communications. It took me eight years to complete this book. What initially began as a self-defence book for women by a woman morphed into how healing happens and why you need a multi-systems approach. The PEMS hygiene model can be practices that anchor you, soothe your nerves, and allow you to come back to an essence you may think is lost. I didn't have a choice when bad things happened in my childhood or when a driver fell asleep at the wheel after having an après ski nightcap and careened into my car. This book teaches you tools to regain agency over your body-mind.

You can now recognize red flags and inappropriate behaviour. You can adopt the strategies for confidence, like Mary did, using her own PEMS routines to fortify herself when her chronic illness weighs her down. Use the tips in this book to reignite your intuition and release limiting beliefs that you inherited. Reminder: Your wounding is not your fault; you are not bad or broken. Rarely have you been taught how to handle the big feelings, how to step away from the circle of chaos, or that you need to step more than once to be successful.

> **Your wounding is not your fault; you are not bad or broken.**

When Sara started training with me, she had a strained relationship with her brother. Every time they tried to connect, the reactivity between them and the larger family unit ignited. After Sara received coaching and spent time in her body, feeling her feelings, she created boundaries so she could safely communicate with him. Her relationship is being nurtured now as opposed to being a drain or a latent source of conflict. She needed coaching and encouragement to feel her feelings and disentangle them from the larger group. Much like a garden hose that has been coiled all winter, when you start to flow in a new direction, without help and traction in that new direction, you can coil back to a reserved state. It is scary to expand away from contraction and pain. It is too easy to stay comfortable even if that comfort is unsafe. You need someone to help notice your positive accomplishments, celebrate your one-degree shifts, and witness the things you do well. It is tricky to notice the positive changes on your own, especially if you have a default pattern of self-minimizing. Working with a trauma-informed somatic coach will guide you back to the essence of you. When you move out of contracted states of being, you move out of the default survival mode that your nervous system is habituated in.

This is where I can help you. Let me be your witness in your healing. You cannot heal in isolation, just like a body never injures itself in isolation. When Amber started working with me, she flat-out said she didn't have any childhood trauma. She was so accustomed to what her reality was and how her body adapted to the stress in her family unit that it never registered that there was patterning she was prey to. It wasn't until she finished my Nerves and Jits program, and saw how her behaviour was a result of the power dynamics in her competitive family, that she could start to make changes. Amber realized that there were gaps in her childhood when her core needs were not met. Though she didn't consider any of it traumatizing, her adult self could see how she developed beliefs and behaviours as a result of those wounded core needs.

Having a coach enabled both of my clients to attune to their needs and release the contracted state. They were able to uncoil their garden hose and feel supported in their expansion. They felt supported to practice autonomy and break the familial conditioning of practiced behaviour that kept them in faulty feedback loops.

Healing is never one-dimensional, it is multi-directional. You need adaptive strategies that evolve alongside you as you heal. The mind is far too clever and can think itself out of feeling really, really easily. Whereas when you are forced to move the body, you FEEL in a different way. It overrides the brain's intellectual response. Your body is so much more than just a flesh suit of muscles and bones. It is a bio-electrical constellation of complicated organizational structures, which includes the housing of your nervous system and your thinking brain. All your components complement and work off of one another. Remember, your brain and your gut are besties, they transmit more information between the two of them than any other system in your body.

The type of Yoga Therapy I teach and the JuJutsu at my academy are adapted to the whole body, irrespective of age, shape or condition. I am potently cognizant that yoga, for most people, conjures up images of acrobatic poses that only flexible people can do. This is misinformation that continues to be promoted by many influencers in the community. Yoga is accessible to everyone and was never intended to solely be represented by the physical form. It is a much, much more nuanced practice that brings to light where you need to develop your PEMS hygiene system. There are many dog-shit yoga classes out there. Therapeutic yoga has been given a bad rap by so many ill-informed teachers, who think laying down and doing twists will heal everyone. You have to be incredibly selective when choosing where to train and who helps you heal.

Trauma-informed jiu-jitsu is amazing at expanding your window of tolerance for stress. You have to learn to live in the suck because the suck is there. It is a moving dance that requires you to develop ongoing skills so that you can anticipate shifts in power. This is not an esoteric philosophy; there will be a literal, physical dance of displacing power from one another as you practice jiu-jitsu. You have to learn how to breathe, how to stay calm, and how to manage the shifts in power from when someone has positional dominance over you to when you have positional dominance over them. On the mat is where you work out some somatic sludge, sweat, feel witnessed, and tap out. Only to show up next time and do it all over again.

If you let the mind lead you, it will be clever and deceptive, defaulting to your negativity bias. Without a teacher, therapist, guide, or coach, this is a tough journey. Let me be your guide! Training yourself to interrupt negative patterns takes time and repetition. I know how deeply ingrained the patterns can be. You do not have to abandon yourself or your needs anymore, dear heart.

I see you.	I see you. I see how strong and capable you are, and I can be here when you forget and when life is too big and loud.

Healing is not a straight line; it is not a one-and-done system. Neither is self-defence. My husband likes to say self-defence skills are perishable. Just like lettuce in your fridge, if you don't use them, they go bad. Rewiring the nervous system and overwriting the negativity bias is the same. Success happens with repetition. Real-world healing is about making little mindset shifts. Repeatedly, continually, over and over again. When healing the nervous system, you always build up gradually towards and into intensity. You must use titration and pendulation to invite the mind and body into new states of safety. Releasing pain points and stored alarms must be done carefully. Your containment for new experiences and new inputs needs to be deliberately built. Please know that you do not enter into a level of healing until you have built up enough capacity in your nervous systems to hold this level of awareness.

This is another thing many instructors get wrong. They are so eager to share tools of enlightenment and devastation but fail to consider that when you are just beginning, you MUST go slowly. I make sure to take great care to not overwhelm you with a high-intensity experience straight out of the gate. So much of learning what a gut punch is, asks you to get into a feeling place, and I REALLY know how hella scary feeling the feelings is!

I know you not only want to heal, but you want to feel safe in the world. You want positive connections with your friends, family, and coworkers. You want attunement with yourself and your desires. You want a secure place to experience love/sexuality, and you want to trust your gut instincts.

You seek autonomy from cultural, societal, and familial programming. I know this because you read my book.

You've been carrying some heavy wounds. Your internal operating system is yearning for a reboot. You're being guided to halt. Pause. Exhale all that tension. Nourish yourself, dear heart.

Start with where you are.

Start with what you've got.

Start with you and your feelings.

The only way you can do this wrong is by not trying.

Acknowledgments

I want to thank all the folks who helped me write this book. First and foremost to the women in my life; the ones who dreamed as big as me, the ones who held space for me, and the ones who showed me that tolerance is not love. That last one was a doozy and lands just right when you heal the nice girl programming.

To Michael Seamark for being my husband, my teacher, my best friend and loyal ride or die. Thank you for helping me feel safe and co-creating a harmonious home. To our children, Kali and Kayma for inspiring me to be my most authentic self and teaching me about unconditional love. Thank you, Leah Morgan, for your steadfast love and friendship over the past 30 years and of course your little cabin that allowed me to be snowed in and write. To my friend Marla Stewart for being my meditation teacher for over 25 years and a kindred spirit, who when together, we become ageless. You introducing me to the concept of bliss and having that space be a reality I can rely upon and trust, is golden.

Thank you to my budo community for challenging and supporting my martial arts career. Specifically, to the feral crew: Shihan Jarrett Mass, Shihan Matt Rodzki, Shihan Avery Yackel. The fires were forged and the iron set during those pivotal years. Arigato Gozaimashita to Soke Irie Yasuhiro for creating KoKoDo JuJutsu. It is a privilege to have access to your teachings. To Chiyokosan Irie, who has beguiling stamina, grace and playfulness and has shown me how to be in a room without taking on all the energy of that room.

I met my buddy Lindsay Whalen in 2007; she was my yoga therapy mentor and she gave me such confidence in my style of teaching and understanding of the practice. We became great friends and colleagues. Thank you Lindsay for introducing me to Judy Daylen and having the perfect writing haven on Salt Spring Island.

To all of my students and clients who showed up on the mat to be witnessed. Your desire to heal and trust this multi directional approach has been an honour to experience with you. Gratitude to Janine Fuller for coaching me into optimal awesomeness. You gave me permission to have boundaries and a reminder to feel joy.

When Dena Morgan offered her time and energy to be my first editor, it unlocked an important block. Giving her my first raw draft was a catalyst to allowing my work to be seen, thank you. To Jason Findlay for editing my book and offering his insight. Thank you to my publisher, Suzanne Doyle-Ingram, who gave me the guidance to start this book in 2018 and who stayed by my side, energetically, until its completion.

My connection to source, to spirit, to the many names I call you: Yesuwa, JC, Mary Magdalene, God, you helped me feel like a wanted daughter and healed my abandonment wounds. I have tremendous gratitude to the wisdom seekers, teachers and healers, in this realm, and to the ones who know they need to show up, do the work and practice radical self compassion.

About the Author

Diane Seamark is a pioneering healer, mentor, and martial artist based in Vancouver, BC. Raised in the West Kootenays, Diane overcame generational trauma to become a leader in holistic wellness and self-empowerment.

Presently, she is the first woman outside of Japan to earn the prestigious Menkyo Kaiden Shihan Kogyoku—a 5th Degree Black Belt in KoKoDo JuJutsu—and one of only two women in the world to hold this rank.

A former nurse turned entrepreneur, Diane co-founded a thriving martial arts and healing center in 1997. Since then, the center has flourished, becoming a trusted hub for personal transformation and community wellness.

Diane's personal healing journey is just as compelling as her professional accomplishments. She has rehabilitated four herniated discs, overcome two autoimmune disorders, and continues to thrive while living with Complex PTSD. Her unique PEMS Hygiene Protocol—focusing on physical, emotional, mental, and spiritual health—serves as the foundation for her work and daily life.

Through her teachings, Diane champions the belief that movement is medicine, self-defence is a fundamental right, and contentment is not something that needs to be earned. She continues to mentor students individually and leads transformative workshops across the globe.

You can find her at:

marysgranddaughter.com

sadohana.com

www.ingramcontent.com/pod-product-compliance
Lightning Source LLC
Chambersburg PA
CBHW071726120626
46550CB00002B/397